fruit
of the
Spirit

THE KINGDOM OF HEAVEN WITHIN

BY LINDA LEA

A book from the Cup of Tea Series

Fruit of the Spirit
The Kingdom of Heaven Within
by Linda Lea

Printed in the United States of America

ISBN 9781629525600

www.xulonpress.com

GRATITUDE

 would like to thank my precious husband Overton who continually supports whatever I am doing. We have been married over twenty-five years now, and the journey just keeps getting better.

Thank you to the children, Jason, Jana, and Warner, (as well as son-in-laws Todd and Chris and daughter—in-law Julie) for continually inspiring me and bringing joy to my heart. I think you are all amazing...and you are wonderful parents to our grandchildren who are exceptional children. Thank you to Chris Turner (my son—in-law) who is a gifted and talented artist for doing the book cover for my book. It is beautiful!

Thank you to my clients and customers who have asked me over and over for a book that contains what I teach them in our visits together. You guys have taught me so much. Our journey together has enriched my life. Your encouragement to write this book has helped it become a reality.

Thanks be to God for His loving mercy that continues to perfect that which concerns us. This perfecting process that He wants us to engage is Him filling us up with Him...helping us to understand that He is calling us to walk in the fullness of the Godhead...to live in that state of abiding that is called oneness. Thank you, Father in Heaven.

CONTENTS

About Linda Lea vii

Introduction ix

Chapter One: The Fruit of the Spirit...a matter of life and death 13

Chapter Two: Kingdom Principles 20

Chapter Three: A Tale of Two Kingdoms 31

Chapter Four: God's Character—the essence of His Kingdom 39

Chapter Five: The Holy Spirit and Communication 43

Chapter Six: The Fruit of the Spirit is Love. 47

Chapter Seven: The Fruit of the Spirit is Joy. 51

Chapter Eight: The Fruit of the Spirit is Peace 58

Chapter Nine: The Fruit of the Spirit is Patience 69

Chapter Ten: The Fruit of the Spirit is Kindness 74

Chapter Eleven: The Fruit of the Spirit is Goodness. 81

Chapter Twelve: The Fruit of the Spirit is Faithfulness 86

Chapter Thirteen: The Fruit of the Spirit is Meekness 90

Chapter Fourteen: The Fruit of the Spirit is Temperance 95

Chapter Fifteen: Acknowledging That We Need Help. 100

Chapter Sixteen: It is Just the Beginning 109

ABOUT THE AUTHOR

Linda Lea
RCR (Registered Certified Reflexologist)
Prayer Ministry, Emotional and Spiritual Empowerment
CCA (Certified Clinical Aromatherapy)
Licensed Aesthetician
Certified Electro-Lymphatic Therapist

*L*inda Lea was called into the intercessory work in her late twenties. That calling was specific to prayer intercession. In her forties, she was called into the intercessory work of being a natural health professional...helping people with their physical challenges. Over the next twenty years, she was made aware of yet another type of intercessory work...that of helping people with emotional and spiritual empowerment processes. At this point in her own journey, she believes that you cannot divide the spiritual, emotional, and physical parts of our being.

Linda's training includes holistic aesthetics, electro-dermal screening (EDS), The Emotion code, Applied Kinesiology, electro-lymphatic therapy, percussion, cold laser, micro-current technology, essential oil science, flower essence therapy, and emotional release and spiritual empowerment facilitation. Linda uses nutritional, herbal, and homeopathic support products to meet client-specific needs and brings therapeutic skin therapies and non-toxic skincare and makeup into her work of holistic aesthetics.

About Lea's Natural Health Solutions, LLC

Lea's Natural Health Solutions, LLC is a place of information and encouragement for those who are on a transformation path. With every service that is provided (health and beauty), the Leas (Overton and Linda) are helping clients understand how the body works and how they can work in harmony with their body. They offer some of the latest natural health assessment tools, leading-edge beauty technology, and pure choices in makeup and skincare.

There is a difference between being well and being whole. It is this difference that Lea's NHS endeavors to help you find.

Overton Lea, BA, MBA, CNC, and Certified GAPS Practitioner is a businessman, Christian writer, and Certified Nutritional Counselor.

Overton manages the operation of Lea's Natural Health Solutions including the extensive inventory of natural health products.

Overton is the author of the soon-to-be-published books, The Beatitudes–A Spiritual Journey, Called By God...Moses and the Exodus, and Called By God...The Prophet Samuel and King Saul. They are true to the Bible as they develop the characters of the people and weave their stories into one continuous thread.

INTRODUCTION

The *Cup of Tea* series includes devotionals, studies, and books. These often pull together science and scripture to make application for our emotional and spiritual healing—our transformation journey. This information introduces the idea of using physical techniques for releasing stored trauma, identifying and releasing the disempowering lies that are sabotaging the transformation journey, and even reprogramming the belief system with the truth of God's word. This is modeled in the Bible, and we have missed it.

We are trained to be spiritually arrogant...thinking that what we know is all that there is to know. This is a fear-based situation and it causes us to call what we do not understand dumb, stupid, or evil. We are cautioned in the Bible not to call that which is of God evil. For this reason, you are encouraged to read <u>Splanka (here let me help) The Redemption of Energy Healing for the Kingdom of God</u> by Sarah J. Thiessen. On my own journey into this arena, it was a faith walk. Now, gratefully, we have science, scripture, and faith coming together in this book.

As a child, my life included abuse on many different levels. In the third grade, someone gave my family a Bible story book. It was lovely. The cover looked like brocade...a deep emerald green brocade...very luxurious for a poor family. No one read that book to me. Given that, it found its way to my bedside and reading it gave me the hope that life could be different. People often ask, "Where was God when I was being hurt?" The green book was God's way of stepping into a wounded child's life. Early on, going to this book about God and the stories of His people became a pattern for me that has helped me throughout my life.

This pattern has developed in me a keen desire to know God's story that is hidden in between the lines. There is wonderful guidance and healing hidden like gems beneath the earth. This understanding is very exciting, and it has taught me that it is in this way that the Bible is an opportunity for relationship with an amazing God, with myself, and with all who walk the planet. Going beneath the surface, it can be discovered that much of what we have been taught about God just does not align correctly with the Word of God. Another personal observation is that mankind has really done a character assassination on God...teaching as commandments the traditions of men.

From the Garden of Eden to the Garden of Gethsemane to an experience of the Garden of Eden being restored, God is for us. He is with us. All those journey companions who tell the stories in the Bible were trying to remind us that in the journey from Eden to Eden, God has not left us nor forsaken us. The journey is not about doing but rather about becoming. It is not about destination. It is about the process of restoration of relationship. Studying the fruit of the Spirit through the lens of relationship changes our goal from doing to being.

It is easy to see the list as something to do through extreme discipline. Discipline and behavior modification, while admirable, are a man-centered, works orientation. They may create an outward change without creating an inward freedom. It is the power of God working through the Holy Spirit to change us from the inside out that will bring us the inward freedom.

"But now being made free from sin, and become servants to God, ye have your fruit unto holiness, and the end everlasting life" *Romans 6:22.*

Enjoy the "fruit" of my labor of love in this study of the fruit of the Spirit. It is a celebration to share this information with you. Knowing that information is not necessarily transformation for any of us, it is with a great deal of humility that this information is presented. Information, in fullest expression, will bring transformation. In its most limited application, it is a seed that can spring to life at its appropriate time.

Chapter 1

WHERE IS MY VICTORY?

Over thirty years ago, God called me into intercessory prayer work. In fact, I did not even know what intercessory prayer was. Yet, one evening around midnight, God pulled me out of bed and gave me a crash course. Over the years, I have studied books, attended seminars and watched DVDs in order to learn more. Through all these, God has taught me this truth—we must know who we are in God before we can understand who we are in relationship with ourselves, others, *and* God. We must have a scriptural foundation for these truths so that everything else aligns with this standard. This is a matter of life and death.

I was introduced to a lady who was struggling with depression. She was on medication; this did not help her. She told me that she did not want to live. Relationship issues had left her wounded and without reserves for regaining herself. I asked her if she had a spiritual practice. She said that she studied the teachings of many different spiritual teachers, but they all seemed to contradict each other.

"How do you know what is true?" she asked. I asked her if she had something–the Bible or something else–that was her standard by which she measured the truth of other teachings. She said no and commented that she just could not embrace the Bible. I explained to her that I, as a Christian, used the Bible as my standard, and that I thought that the Bible had much to say about a recovery process for our brokenness. I offered to share some of those ideas with her if she wanted to know more.

Perhaps out of courtesy or curiosity, she accepted the offer. I had one appointment with her where I introduced to her God's recovery process from the Bible. I offered to continue visiting with her if she wanted to explore further. She thanked me, but never called for another appointment. Later, I learned that she had committed suicide. This is a tragic story that illustrates well the importance of answering for yourself her question...How do you know what is true?

Because she was not a Christian, it is far too easy for us to think that her story is an isolated case. Given that, I meet regularly with Christian people who are struggling with unresolved emotional and spiritual issues and the resulting depression and anxiety. They say to me, "I have prayed about this over and over. Where is my victory?" Praise God! We are asking the correct question. I have observed that all "flavors" of Christians are asking this question. I wonder if perhaps this is the major Christian dilemma right now. I see Christians who have participated in deliverance ministries in an effort to find freedom. Some have been prayed over in prayer ministry sessions. They come away confused and despondent because "victory" was not the consequence of these efforts. Some get a temporary relief from their emotional and spiritual crises only to have it resurface days later.

Praying over someone to be healed or freed from depression or anxiety without that person engaging in a process that uncovers the lies that they believe is a violation of a person's free will. Zoning in on the behavior is not the place to begin. The behavior is a symptom. We must understand that the behavior is there because of a belief/lie. We need to go to the root belief and get freedom by replacing the lie with truth. We need to move from victim mode to being willing to be accountable and responsible for our health on all levels—mind, body, spirit.

Some people do not want to be inconvenienced by any life-style changes. People are usually happy with their life-style (or see no way to change it). However, we are uncomfortable with the consequences of that life-style. We just want the discomfort to go away. Many times a person has not put it together that life-style and physical, emotional, and spiritual health have anything to do with each other.

In my own experience in my early forties, I was very sick. I had been diagnosed with five or six very unpleasant syndromes and autoimmune processes. I asked to be anointed and prayed over. This was done. I did not, however, get well. When I asked God about it, He said, "Linda, if I heal you today with how you are living your life and with what you are carrying, I will have to heal you in two weeks."

Basically, God was saying to me, "Linda, go and sin no more, and you will be healed as you go." I knew the truth of what God was saying. I was overdoing, over-committing, under-eating, overworking...I was a crazy, dysfunctional, codependent who had crashed and burned. It was time for me to "go and sin no more." I was destroying God's temple while thinking that all my good efforts were building up the kingdom of God. Incongruent! I know that I am not the only crazy Christian behaving this way. Yet, we go to church each week and everyone is "just fine." We all have on our going-to-church smiley faces while inside of us we feel defeated, depressed, and even suicidal. We need help.

Unfortunately, the help we need is not coming from the church because our society fractures us into the physical, the emotional, and the spiritual...and there is an expert for each part and often the "whole" is not considered. This fracturing is disempowering to us, and we buy hook, line,

15

and sinker that someone else is smarter and "responsible" for helping us. We go, not to Scripture first for our help, but to a specialist. In part, this failure comes from a lack of Biblical instruction on the foundational truths about God and relationship living with God and man. As in Jeremiah's time, we now find "each man doing what is right in his own eyes." Man-centered, works-oriented teachings and therapies have replaced the word of God.

As Christians, we have embraced the cross of Christ. We are eager to receive the blessing of this work. For the dying daily part of sanctification, however, we seem to have less knowledge and understanding. This is the process that helps us make application of the word of God for obtaining the victory in our lives. In regard to the "how to" of overcoming through the word, one lady told me that she had often heard from the pulpit that we need to overcome, but never in her experience had she heard anyone give instruction or guidance on the how-to of overcoming.

"Through these he has given us his very great and precious promises,
so that through them you may participate in the divine nature and
escape the corruption in the world caused by evil desires." 2 Peter 1:4

Several times a week, I talk with Christian people, young and old, who really do not understand what the Bible says about who they are in Christ and who Christ is in them. Nor do they have a clear perception of what the Earth School journey is all about. Even with a basic theological understanding, many people have not been taught how to make a daily application of Scripture, and this is the key for victory.

What is victory? What does it look like? What does it taste like? How does it feel? Modified behavior, while admirable, is not victory. It is a man-centered, works orientation. It is a fig-leaf garment that we have made because shame pushes us to cover ourselves. Correct understanding regarding the life issues connected with being on a spiritual journey through the Earth School experience is essential. Inappropriate expectations about life, God, self, and others factor in to much of the depression, anxiety, and other relationship issues that everyone is dealing with including Christians. Understanding is one part of the process, and we cannot forget the heart and emotions. How do we put it all together? How do we stop being double minded and become congruent?

This study started out to be *simply* a study of the fruit of the Spirit. There is *simply nothing simple* about the fruit of the Spirit. Over the months of study, life of course, has happened. These life experiences have been viewed with eyes that are looking at life through the lens of the fruit of the Spirit. This truly changes everything.

For example, I was in a gathering and someone I only slightly know started making some comments. As I listened, my stomach went into a knot. Now, viewing this through the lens of the fruit of the Spirit, I had to say to God that I did not feel His Spirit within. Praying silently, I asked God to show me the reason for this reaction. He impressed me with the truth that I was responding to this person's spiritual immaturity. He said that my reaction was not about that person, but was connected to a responsibility issue for which I was seeking freedom. The reaction was about an internal dysfunctional program that demanded that in some way it is my responsibility to "save" people from themselves and the things they believe that are hindering their emotional and spiritual growth.

There is a fine line between being evangelistic and obnoxious, and I sometimes cross that line! It makes my stomach hurt. Viewed through the lens of the fruit of the Spirit, I was able to ask God to remove this dysfunctional programming in my heart, mind, and gut. Using prayer and a simple physical technique, God changed my programming and gave me victory.

Within a few minutes, the same person was again making comments, and I felt absolutely nothing negative in my stomach. Praise the Lord!

A favorite text puts this into perspective: *"But if we walk in the light, as He is in the light, we have fellowship one with another, and the blood of Jesus Christ His Son cleanseth us from all sin 1 John 1:8."* God has promised to reveal truth to us. He shows us the light about ourselves. The amazing and comical aspect of this is that God has linked fellowship with one another and being cleansed by the blood of Jesus!

In any occasion for fellowship of any sort, there is the opportunity of being around someone who just is not your favorite person. Viewing this challenge through the lens of the fruit of the Spirit, it can be seen that God is using people who are not our "favorites" to show us something about ourselves. He shows us where are wounds are. That is humbling, isn't it? Our wounds and the resulting grudges, bitterness, shame, guilt, etc., create blocks that cause physical, emotional, and spiritual sickness. We get stuck in these places because we do not understand that they are God's messengers trying to convict us of truth and repentance and forgiveness.

This chapter has embraced a very BIG picture of life and death issues. Are we victims or are we victorious? The mind/body/spirit connection cannot be ignored for any part affects the other. Science is now saying that it is the thoughts that are regulating the cellular activity of the body.

"Casting down imaginations, and every high thing that exalteth itself against the knowledge of God and bringing into captivity every thought to the obedience of Christ" 2 Corinthians 10:5. As we use God's word as the standard by which we measure everything in our lives, we will discover that we are all living fractured lives with different sets of rules for different arenas. We are even living and reacting by rules of which we are unaware. This reality means that we must be kind and gentle to ourselves and to our fellows on the journey.

The word of God is being validated by science. As Christians, I am afraid we are not aware of this. Science is telling us that ninety percent of our physical distresses have an emotional trigger. The Bible says that as a man thinks in his heart so is he. We are told that the tongue has the power of life and death. How are we applying these life-altering scriptures to our lives? Doctors of acupuncture often see that when they use the acupuncture points in their treatments, people have an emotional release. The trauma, the emotional pain has been stored in the body, and physical techniques can clear them. We have the knowledge now of how to utilize our bodies to help heal emotional, spiritual, and physical distresses. I believe that this is also modeled in the Bible.

Chapter 2

FIRST THINGS FIRST

Honestly, I have often been a bit overwhelmed when I looked at the list of the fruit of the Spirit. For one thing, I did not know where to begin. We just do not seem to be able to wake up one morning and start loving as Christ loves. Who can do that? Being somewhat analytical, I wondered if there might be some significance to the order of the fruit. I know that God means what He says, and that often the order of His lists is an invitation to go deeper into study. For instance, in II Timothy 1:7: *"For God hath not given us the spirit of fear; but of power, and of love, and of a sound mind."* Notice that fear is the extreme opposite of a sound mind. I do not think this coincidental..

The reason I have had trouble understanding the fruit is because I was looking at the list as something to do rather than something to become as a consequence of God's work in me. With this new perspective, the order of the fruit makes a great deal of sense to me. Another point of confusion for me with this study is this: If the fruit is the goal, where am I now and how do I get to the goal? Jumping into the middle of the list left me feeling somewhat like I was treading water while looking for some place firm upon which I could plant my feet. This pushed me to review the work of the Holy Spirit as outlined in the Bible.

- Convict the world of guilt in regard to sin (John 16:8)
- Convert the sinner (John 3:5-9)
- Cleanse the Christian (Galatians 5:22 – 23)
- Commission the Christian for service (1 Corinthians 12 and 14: receiving the gifts of the Holy Spirit)
- Communicate with the Christian (Romans 8)

Christians have eagerly embraced the cross of Christ. This is the convicting and converting part of the Spirit's work. Sometimes this is called the first love experience. We also find modeled in Scripture the other steps (cleansing, communicating, commissioning) of the Spirit's work. This is what Paul called the dying daily part of the Christian experience. The abiding experience or the sanctification process are other names describing the dynamics of being filled with the fruit of the Spirit.

It is estimated that only about twenty percent of Christians enter into the work of cleansing with the Holy Spirit. This is accomplished by paying attention to personal fellowship, quiet time, communication, and an active devotional life day by day. The Holy Spirit is not pushy. We must ask for the Spirit, and give Him permission to do this work. He persistently urges us, but He will not go against our will. Of what is the Spirit cleansing us? The works of the flesh. We will look at that a bit later. They are opposites. It is the fruit of the Spirit that replaces the "flesh."

Before we begin to look specifically at the fruit of the Spirit, let us partner these two texts:

- *Romans 14:17: For the kingdom of God is not meat and drink but righteousness, peace, and joy in the Holy Ghost.*

- *Matthew 23:26: ...cleanse first that which is within the cup and platter, that the outside of them may be clean also.*

Righteousness, peace and joy are some of the fruit of the Holy Spirit. Jesus, when talking to the Pharisees in Matthew 23, called them "blind" because they were more concerned with the outside than the inside. Jesus is telling us that we are not wholly clean unless there is an inside work done. The fruit of the Holy Spirit is God's character taking up residence in our heart and mind. These verses are saying then that the fruit of the Holy Spirit creates the kingdom of God within you. So the kingdom is both a place "Heaven" and an internal work; it is the work of grace upon the heart. You can study the kingdom parables and understand this more clearly.

This thought enhances the understanding of what the Holy Spirit is doing in this "cleansing" work of infilling God's people with His character...the fruit of the Spirit...His work of sanctification. To me, this information changes the entire dynamic of the fruit of the Spirit. This is not something I practice. This is a relationship into which I enter fulfilling John 17:21–23:

"That they all may be one as thou, Father, art in me, and I in thee, that they also may be one in us; that the world may believe that thou hast sent me. And the glory which thou gavest me I have given them; that they may be one, even as we are one. I in them, and thou in me, that they may be made perfect in one, and that the world may know that thou hast sent me, and hast loved them, as thou has loved me."

Purpose: that the world may believe that God has sent the Son, and the world may know that God sent Christ and loves them as He loves Christ. Here is Heaven's amazing agenda! We each must believe in Christ.

We each must know that God sent Christ. We each must experience that God loves **us just as He loves Christ.**

God needs a people who can witness to the power of the Holy Spirit within. The oneness we have with the Godhead changes our witness. When you realize that most Christians do not believe (less than forty percent) that the Holy Spirit is a living force making a difference in our lives, you understand the significance of God needing to have witnesses to the world (The Barna Group Survey, 4/2009). According to a Gallop poll conducted in June of 2007, fifty-four percent of Americans stated that the church has no credibility.

God needs witnesses. If we have no personal story of what God has done for us, all we have to give people is doctrine. That does not save. Not only does the world need a witness, but it looks like the church needs witnesses to the difference that God makes in our lives. It is this indwelling of the power of Heaven that comes to our aid in the struggles of the flesh mentioned by Paul. This is God's way of moving us back towards His original creation purpose that according to Romans 8 is to *"be conformed to the image of His Son."*

Notice in the above John 17 quotation that it says: *the glory which thou gavest me I have given them; that they may be one, even as we are one.* Let us look at the word "glory." Remember the story of Moses asking to see God? Exodus 33:18: *"And he (Moses) said, I beseech thee, show me thy glory."* How did God respond? Verse 19: *"I will make all my goodness pass before thee, and I will proclaim the name of the Lord before thee..."*

God told Moses that it was impossible to see God's face and live, but that Moses could see God's "back parts". This is like saying that Moses could see where God had been. When you look at Exodus 34:6 – 7, there is a description of God's glory. All of the words that describe His glory are the same words that are descriptive of the fruit of the Spirit. It is the character of God that is called His glory. It is this "glory" that Christ said he received from God and gives to us. Amazing! The glory of God is the fruit of the Spirit. The fullness of God's character/glory is that to which we are called in Ephesians 3:19: *"...that ye might be filled with all the fullness of God."*

Fruit is something that develops as a consequence of being connected to something else. Fruit bearing is controlled by the main plant/vine/tree. That spark of divine planning that sets in motion life and by which life is sustained is responsible for the development of fruit. In the story that Jesus told about the vine and branches, we discover some important concepts.

- Fruit bearing follows growth and development
- Fruit only develops if it remains attached
- The fruit is food for those who are hungry
- The fruit are not responsible for the pruning.

Pruning: There are at least two ways of looking at the pruning process. One, the branches are symbolic of more than one person. Or, two, that the branches are symbolic of one person. I think that it is allowable to have the parable cover both scenarios. Pruning is a part of the care and keeping of the plant. Pruning helps the development of the fruit. From the point of view that the branches are more than one person...say a group of people like Laodicea...then pruning can be seen as a type of judgment. It is the non-productive branches that must be pruned away.

From the standpoint of the branches being aspects of one person, then the pruning can mean that the non-productive tendencies, our dysfunctional patterns of living, our struggle with the flesh, etc. are being pruned away. This is the application that I want to make. This is the dying daily that Paul talks about. In this case, it is not a "final" judgment scene. It is a judgment that is an intimate getting to know ourselves in the light of

God's wisdom and coming into agreement (holiness) with Him regarding our conscious and subconscious motivations and dysfunctions. This type of judgment brings us to the place of being willing to allow him to write the law on our hearts and minds. *"If we would judge ourselves, we would not need to be judged..." 1 Corinthians 11:31.*

It is a trimming and burning (purifying) of that which is slowing down the development of fruit: the development of God's glory in us. There is the "burning" of the trimmed/pruned branches that can be equated with the gold tried in the fire; the gold of faith surfacing as a consequence of trusting God with the pruning process. How does God do His pruning work? We need to know this so we can cooperate with Him. I discovered that often I was fighting against His efforts because they made be uncomfortable.

I have a little room that I use for my at-home chapel. I love that little room. I was thinking about my time in my chapel, and I realized that the battle to stay focused is not a battle at all. It is an opportunity from God. Whatever comes into my mind is because it is seeking to be higher than my thoughts of God. I would not know this if they did not show up. So, God uses even my distractions to help me see the truth that this thing, whatever or whoever it is, is competing for a place on God's throne. I used to fight against these thoughts trying to push them down. Suppression is not freedom. Now, I acknowledge them and use a physical technique on the hands to release them. It is awesome. The mind, body, spirit connection responds well to this type of process.

The more we get rid of this stuff, the more we can glorify God as a "cup" that has been cleaned on the inside...as Jesus said to the Pharisees. The mind gets quiet, and the heart grows peaceful and grateful. Instead of spending my time fighting these things, I can now learn life lessons from my time in my chapel. I am recording these thoughts and lessons and will make them available in the book <u>From the Chapel</u> as soon as it is ready. If we remember that those things with which we are struggling are an invitation from God to embrace healing rather than something we fight against, it changes everything. What we fight against we empower.

In Galatians 5:19 – 26: the works of flesh and the fruit of the Spirit are listed one after the other. It is interesting that in the flesh, these are called "works". The spiritual path, however, acknowledges that these characteristics are the fruit of the Spirit that are developed in us as a consequence of aligning ourselves with the Spirit and His work for us. In Philippians 2:12 and 13 we are told to *"...work out your own salvation with fear and trembling. For it is God which worketh in you both to will and to do of His good pleasure."*

I am grateful for verse 13 that says that it is God who works in us to will and to do. This is a work that partners the Divine with the human. God places within us the will and ability to be and do and thereby fulfill His good pleasure in us. What is our part? How do we "work out" our own salvation with fear and trembling? If the Divine part of the plan is the willing and doing, then the human part of the effort is verse 14: *"Do everything without grumbling and arguing, so that you may be blameless and pure, children of God who are faultless in a crooked and perverted generation, among whom you shine like stars in the world."*

This type of "doing" invites us to come up to a higher place and view the work of Divine transformation from Heaven's eyes. This is the only possible way we can "not" grumble and argue. When we grumble and argue, we have made a judgment about something or someone. Judge not, that ye be not judged. Our text says not to grumble and argue (judge) so that we may be blameless and pure, children of God who are faultless. If we are judging, we shall be judged...therefore, we are not blameless, pure, and faultless.

Couple this thought with 1 John 1:17: *"But if we walk in the light as He Himself is in the light, we have fellowship with one another, and the blood of Jesus His Son cleanses us from all sin."* What fellowship does light have with darkness? None. A favorite writer, A. W. Tozer, in his book <u>Pursuit of God</u>, gives an example of tuning pianos. He says that if you try to tune a room full of pianos to each other, they will never be in tune. If, however, you tune each piano to one piano, they will all be in tune with each other.

You see, the light in which we need to fellowship is that Light which is Jesus and His word. These have cleansing potential. How do we make such a transition? It truly does take Divine intervention, and that is via the work of the Holy Spirit in changing us from our image into Christ's image. So often, we want other people to be changed into our image. If this were not true, then we would not be upset with others when they do things that we do not like! We would not react negatively when others have an opinion that is different than ours. A basic thing to remember is that we are to seek first the Kingdom of God and His righteousness. This leaves no room for seeking our kingdoms, or the kingdoms of others, or self-righteousness from a man-centered, works orientation.

In Job 42:10, we are told that the LORD turned the captivity of Job, when he prayed for his friends: also the LORD gave Job twice as much as he had before. Remember, the "friends" were those folks that God said had lied about Him. The words that these "friends" spoke were accusations and condemnation. This, of course, is not the spirit of God. It comes from the the accuser of the brethren. This is such an important concept to get. So much of what we say about God will be a "lie" if we are not grounded in the truth of God's word. These people misunderstood the character of God, and, therefore, their assessment of Job's time of trouble was inaccurate and was distressing to Job.

Like Job, our captivity can be turned when we pray for others who have hurt us. God knew that these people had very much distressed Job. He knew that it was just as important to Job that he pray for these "friends" as it was for the friends to be prayed for, and I am sure forgiven. This is another example of how the fruit of the Spirit can be developed in our life as we deal with difficult people and situations. So often, we want the fruit without the effort. We want the purity without the purification process. None of us really like coming to the truth that what we see in others that we dislike or criticize is a reflection of that which is in our own hearts. Ouch!

Usually, when disturbed by something or someone, we kick into judgment, criticism, and blame. None of this will bring us freedom. These are really opportunities for overcoming. Listed below are a few of the principles that can help us measure everything that happens by a different standard. There are many more.

- That which you fight against, you empower.
- If you spot it, you have got it.
- What disturbs me is showing me something about me.
- Lies about non-disturbance, for instance: if they change, I will be happy; if I change, they will be happy, etc.
- Authority issues

We are blessed that there are many physical processes that help us to address total body healing. I have studied many of them and find value in all of them. Even the Jewish davening (prayer) in which you see the person putting a hand on the forehead and the back of the neck is creating an emotional release for the person praying in this manner. It is engaging what is called the neuro-emotional holding points of the body. It is also engaging the acupuncture systems that have been shown to facilitate emotional release.

I discovered on my own journey, that I had totally intellectualized my child abuse. I had talked it to death, but my physiology was still being negatively impacted. A part of my physical healing came from using physical techniques that eliminated stored emotions. My prayer has been consistently, "Lord, restore me to your original intent...that which I was meant to be before mankind had a chance to mess things up." I praise God that He is faithful in restoring what the locust has eaten! He delivers us because He delights in us.

This chapter and the next one help us to know where we are and where we are going. Otherwise, the list of the fruit of the Spirit will seem just like another checklist that we need to incorporate into our day. We need to enter into this faith-based, God-centered process that is not about doing, but rather about becoming. I see so many people who are trying to "do" the correct things in regard to their health. Given that, they are not getting well. Why? Because the mind, body, spirit connection is not being honored. They just keep changing doctors or natural health practitioners. For all the time and expense they put into it, they are still sick.

One day, I had a lady come for help with allergies. I tend to believe that allergies are a symptom of something else. I do energetic allergy testing, and she showed some sensitivity. However, when I tested her against the allergen and an emotional remedy, she did not test sensitive. This means that the allergy/sensitivity is triggered by something emotional.

Using muscle response testing, I was able to determine that she believed that it was not safe to be well. She actually had what is referred to as a death wish. Combining prayer and an energetic clearing technique, we were able to remove this programming from her. She no longer tested sensitive to certain foods. Better than that, she tested that she was free from the self-hate which was driving the death wish. Physically, she could feel the difference

Bruce Lipton is a research biologist and a pioneer in the field of epigenetics, the study of how gene expression is altered by causes other than DNA. Dr. Lipton tells us that science is now proving that the our thoughts change our DNA...for good or bad. It has been validated in the science lab that down to the cellular level our body is responding to our beliefs. The process of combining prayer with physical techniques embraces the totality of who we are...even our beliefs. Scripture tells us that as a man thinks, so is he. This is powerful. We have these profound principles in the Bible, and we have not understood that they are laws of nature...our nature...mind, body, and spirit. Would you be whole? I believe in the power of this whole-body approach.

Chapter 3

A TALE OF TWO KINGDOMS

"Know ye not, that to whom ye yield yourselves servants to obey, his servants ye are to whom ye obey; whether of sin unto death, or of obedience unto righteousness." **Romans 6:16**

There are two kingdoms at war. The attributes of these kingdoms are listed in Galatians 5. These are listed below.

The Fruit of the Spirit

Love, joy, peace, longsuffering, patience, kindness, goodness, faith, meekness, temperance/self-control

The Works of the Flesh

Adultery, fornication, uncleanness, lasciviousness, idolatry, witchcraft, hatred, variance, emulations, wrath, strife, seditions, heresies, envy, murders, drunkenness, reveling

Studying these attributes from the standpoint that they are actually two opposing Spirits and kingdoms may help us understand what is at stake in the war. The above scripture from Romans tells us that whomever we obey, to that Spirit we are servants either for life or death. When we look at the two lists in Galatians 5, it would be wonderful if we did not recognize ourselves in some of these works of the flesh. It is so easy to judge the sins of others as worse than ours, especially when they are sexual sins. Given that, those sins are in the same list as hatred, strife, jealousy, anger, dissensions, factions, envy, drunkenness, and carousing.

Putting this into perspective, we approve of these very things when we watch TV shows and/or movies and/or game playing that portray these behaviors. See Romans 1:32: by watching, we are applauding Hollywood. We participate in these works of the flesh, even if vicariously. We must be actively engaged in the process of the Spirit's cleansing, and by beholding we are changed. Galatians 5:16: *"I say then, walk by the Spirit and you will not carry out the desire of the flesh."* The only way we can stay out of the works of the flesh is if we *"walk by the Spirit."*

These "works" of the flesh can be the open door, or legal right, that Satan uses to establish his territory and to begin building his kingdom within. For instance, a lack of forgiveness is an open door through which Satan can establish one of his strongholds or a root of bitterness. These strongholds create a fear of the same and sets in motion rejection of self, others, and even an unconscious programming that causes us to put ourselves over and over again into situations where rejection will happen. Rejection creates defensiveness. There are many "defensive" strategies.

Romans 6:16 moves us into the issue of spiritual authority. Unless we daily place ourselves under the authority of Heaven, we will be under the authority and rule of the other kingdom. There is no middle ground. *"And if it seem evil unto you to serve the LORD, choose you this day whom ye will serve; whether the gods which your fathers served that were on the other side of the flood, or the gods of the Amorites, in whose land ye dwell: but as for me and my house, we will serve the LORD" Joshua 24:15.* Understanding spiritual authority is an important key in daily victory. We know that Christ was subject to the Father, and in Ephesians 5 we see that Christ is the head of the church. We also see that the husband is head of the wife. If drawn out, this would look like the following:

Spiritual Authority
- God and the Holy Spirit
- Jesus
- Government
- Church universal
- Local church and pastor
- Husband
- Parents

You may ask why it is that "government" is listed between Jesus and the church. This is because today's churches have signed an agreement with the government for tax exempt status. That puts the government over the church for good or for evil.

The issue of spiritual authority is very important. If a husband does not love his wife as Christ loves the church (abuse, addiction, adultery, etc.), he has abandoned his right to be her spiritual covering. If he has abandoned this right, then the relationship does not exist in the spiritual realm. This creates a great deal of difficulty for a wife who is trying to be faithful to an unfaithful husband. His sins become open doors that the devil successfully uses to bring damage to the wife and children. That husband's sins (choices) will play out in the family. The consequence is the setting up spiritual strongholds in the wife and children.

Another example: If a pastor refuses to be under the authority of Jesus (being Biblically grounded in all his ways), that pastor has abandoned his right to be spiritual head over a flock of God's children. The devil is a legalist and understands authority. Although God might like to intervene, the pastor who is not aligning himself with truth is opening a door for the devil to come in and create great havoc within the church. Those church members who stay in that church hoping that it will get better are also opening themselves up to spiritual havoc to work out in their lives. They are aligning themselves with someone who is not aligned with God.

An example of this is the situation where a pastor had abandoned his alignment with God and refused to step down as pastor. The church began to be in great turmoil: power struggles, emotional upsets, loss of membership, loss of offerings, etc. The pastor's unfaithfulness to Christ represents a type of spiritual adultery. This opened up this church to that type of stronghold and, as a consequence, there was more than one church member that was involved in an adulterous relationship within the church membership. This is so sad.

The betrayal of spiritual authority opens a door for Satan. It gives him permission to manifest the works of the flesh in the lives of those who have aligned themselves with the kingdom of darkness. The spirit of evil begins to work like leaven in the lives of those who are in darkness creating spiritual strongholds in their own lives and the lives of those over whom they may have some power. The issue of spiritual strongholds is an important topic. These strongholds can come as a consequence of our own sins, the sins of others against us, and even as a consequence of a belief, behavior, or tendency or attitude that has come through the family via the modeling from parents or other family members.

When a child suffers some type of abuse, that child is likely to internalize that abuse as rejection and self-hate. As the child grows up, this internalized rejection will lead to rejection of self, rejection of others, and rejection of God. Rejection, grief, suppressed anger, abandonment issues and so many other strongholds change the course of a person's life. Below is a chart that defines the works of the flesh from Strong's Concordance.

These definitions help us see that we are all too often living out the works of the flesh in our lives.

Just as the fruit of the Spirit fill us with God's spirit, the works of the flesh represent an evil spirit that seeks to indwell in God's temple. This is about so much more than an occasional inappropriate act. Again, it is about choosing under whose authority we will live. In 1 Peter 1:13-16 we are told *to "gird up the loins of your mind, be sober, and hope to the end for the grace that is to be brought unto you at the revelation of Jesus Christ; ...As obedient children, not fashioning yourselves according to the former lusts in your ignorance: But as he which hath called you is holy, so be ye holy in all manner of conversation; Because it is written, Be ye holy; for I am holy."*

It is the revelation of Jesus Christ that brings us into a place of grace. This revelation, the Word of God, is the standard by which we measure all things. He is our place of overcoming. Heaven's initiative for us, the Lamb slain from the foundation of the earth, has given us back the rights that we gave away in the garden. When Satan said, *"ye shall not surely die,"* he was lying. It was the first lie. The translation of Enoch and Elijah can give us much hope. They lived their lives so filled with Holy Spirit power (the fruit of the Spirit) that obedience was natural. The wages of sin is death. They were obedient, and, therefore, could not be brought under the dominion of death. Let these words be encouragement for each of us.

Our wounds from living in a sinful world (abuse, rejection, fear, anger, grief, shame, guilt, etc.) become the open doors through which Satan takes up residence and continues to develop his kingdom through the works of the flesh. Listed below is a short study on the spirit of the enemy. Unfortunately, we all will find ourselves somewhere on this list.

Work of the flesh, Strong's Concordance Definition

Adultery	These first 4 have to do with idolatry, indulgence in unlawful lust of either sex, and including adultery and incest. These works can manifest in the flesh or in the mind, and represent spiritual adultery to God.
Fornication	
Uncleanness	
Lasciviousness	
Idolatry	(1495) worship of an image or god other than God
Witchcraft	(5331 from 5332) pharmakeia from the word for drugs, medication, pharmacy, spell-promoting potion, magic, sorcery, witchcraft. It was long part of pagan religious practice to administer potions, or drugs, which would encourage hallucinations. It is never used in a positive light. Its background is based in the pagan use of mind-altering drink and drugs combined with temple prostitution and child sacrifice. Pagan religions were based on lies perpetuated by practices that offered only temporary escapes from reality. As soon as their drugged stupor wore off, they were back to feeling like they did before the potion had been taken. They became addicted to the potions as well as the processes.
Hatred	(2189) hostility, opposition, enmity, from 2190 to hate, hateful, usually a noun, an adversary, enemy, foe, Satan
Variance	(2054) quarrel, contention, debate, strife
Emulations	(2205) jealousy (as of a husband)
Wrath	(2372) fierceness, indignation, wrath
Strife	(2052) faction, intrigue, provoke
Seditions	(1370) dissension, division
Heresies	(139) undermining what is, trying to replace
Envyings	(5355) ill will, spite, to spoil, ruin (jealousy wants; envy destroys if it cannot have)
Murders	(5408) to slay
Drunkenness	(3178) an intoxicant, intoxication
Revelings	(2970) letting loose, rioting

We are living in a time like Jeremiah's where every man does what is right in his own eyes. Christians themselves are misrepresenting the God of Heaven. Many people will not consider even going to church or becoming a Christian because there is so little "fruit" in evidence. I hear Christians talking about things that sound true or feel good. Something can sound true and not be truth. Something can feel good and not be Biblical. Experience must be validated by Biblical truth, Isaiah 8:20: *"If they speak not according to this word, it is because there is NO light in them."* This is a strong scripture, and if we align ourselves with it, we will remain not only safe but humble in regards to our own opinions.

We need to be able to recognize true from false. We need our personal "programming" to be based on the Word of God. *"Know ye not, that to whom ye yield yourselves servants to obey, his servants ye are to whom ye obey; whether of sin unto death, or of obedience unto righteousness"* Romans 6:16.

In studying the battle between good and evil, it is well to note a primary concept of forgiveness. In the midst of the battle, as Jesus hung on the cross, He said, *"Father, forgive them for they know not what they do"* Luke 23:34. Forgiveness (forgiving ourselves, forgiving God, forgiving others) is the doorway to all healing. In Matthew 6:12, the Lord's prayer models the principle of forgiveness; forgiving others as we are forgiven. In my own life and the lives of others with whom I have prayed, I have observed that a lack of forgiveness may keep us from hearing from God. I have seen Christians so weighed down with hate and revenge towards someone who hurt them, that nothing they do in "ministry" for God is successful.

A lady came into my office one day for her appointment. She was in pain all over her body. As I visited with her, it became evident that she was very angry with her church and people in her church. I asked her if we could pray about this situation and ask for God's guidance. She agreed. We prayed. She did not hear from God.

I told her that anger can sometimes cause us to not hear from God. I asked if she would be willing to set aside her anger...just pretend that she could collect it all from her body and put it somewhere else for a while. She was very willing to do this. Then we prayed again, and she received the answer that she needed for healing, and we talked about forgiving based simply on "Father, forgive them for they know not what they are doing." In other words, we are all "ignorant" when it comes to what we are doing that hurts each other. We are also "ignorant" of the lens through which we perceive life situations. This lens causes us to interpret things incorrectly.

She was so delighted, and when I reminded her that she could have her anger back if she still wanted it. Very emphatically she declined to take it back. The interesting thing about this experience is that when she came in she was in massive pain. When she left, there was no pain in her body.

Our sins and the sins of others against us, are open doors that the Devil uses to establish his "spirit" within us. Those spirits include rejection, anger, hate/murder, grief, fear, etc. Forgiveness work is a door that opens us up to God's Spirit. We want to close the door to Satan, and open the door to God. A lack of forgiveness sets us up for the works of the flesh to manifest. As we look at the list, we can easily see that the church is full of these "spirits". When we have ill will, gossip, envy, jealousy, power struggles causing hurt to others, we are allowing these "spirits" to move us to the killing of relationships. That is another type of murder.

Praise be to God that we have a way out and that He has given us such specific instruction on how to be victorious in Him. We are not victims in this battle. We are co-conquerors with Christ. We get to help vindicate God showing that He is both just and the justifier (Romans 3:26). What an amazing God we have!

Chapter 4

GOD'S CHARACTER...THE ESSENCE OF HIS KINGDOM

*A*ny of these chapters could be a book on its own. I have no grand illusions that I am dong justice to a particular subject. I want to bring a big-picture point-of-view, and into that interject some new thoughts and a different way of making application of a particular scripture. I want it to encompass the emotions. I want it to challenge our beliefs. Our behavior is based on our beliefs! With this awareness, let us leave the works of the flesh and look into the beautiful spirit of God. The Fruit of the Spirit is listed below:

- Love
- Joy
- Peace
- Long-suffering/Patience
- Kindness
- Goodness
- Faith
- Meekness
- Temperance/Self-control

Sometimes we can best understand what something is by seeing what it is not. This may be helpful in a study of the fruit of the Spirit. I see the specific fruit as a positive while its extreme opposite is a negative that will manifest as a work of the flesh. For instance, a lack of peace might manifest as selfish ambition or envy, or some of the other works of the flesh. It is important to understand that we can move from a positive place into negative places by disengaging the work of the Holy Spirit.

This can happen, too, with the gifts of the Holy Spirit. You have probably met people who use their gift of discernment as a weapon with which to injure others, and they believe that this is a God-calling for their lives. Father, forgive us, for we do not know what we are doing.

The opposite of love may be thought of as hate or rage. However, the opposite of love can also be indifference. Indifference might actually be worse than hate or rage. With these there is at least an emotion attached. Indifference, however, is non-emotional. It just does not matter. Another opposite of love is indulgence. When we indulge someone to the point of hampering their emotional and spiritual maturity, we are not loving them as God loves. As hard as it may be, God allows us to face the consequences of our choices.

This is an interesting dynamic, however, because sometimes people use "tough love" to protect their own interest at the expense of someone who has been put into their sphere of influence so that both parties may learn something. Knowing when to disengage or when to keep on keeping on is definitely only something the Holy Spirit can show you. *"However, when He, the Spirit of truth, has come, He will guide you into all truth" John 16:13.*

First Corinthians 13, the love chapter, gives us another perspective on love. Sometimes what looks like love is actually motivated by something else...perhaps the need to find significance in doing and being seen. Our giving and doing becomes nothing more than a business transaction when that which motivates us is our own brokenness and neediness. Again, it takes the Holy Spirit's guidance to see ourselves as we truly are.

This leads us easily into the concept of maturity before ministry. God can and does use us all even while we are spiritually immature. So, I am not suggesting that we sit around waiting for perfection. It is really amazing what God can accomplish with a group of broken and wounded saints who have not yet learned that it is not all about them and the works of their own hands.

We chose in the beginning to "know good and evil." God must allow us to learn from the consequences of the choices we make, and hopefully learn that our ways are not His ways. *"For My thoughts are not your thoughts, neither are your ways My ways, saith the Lord"* Isaiah 55:8. We like to think that this truth is for other people, so we push our own agenda in all our spheres of influence including the church because, after all, it is a good agenda.

Have you ever engaged in a battle about something or for someone only to come away from it looking like the bad guy? Have you discovered that you have fought some battles that no one asked you to fight? As a matter of fact, maybe you have discovered that you seem to care more than anyone else about the issue(s). Sometimes we even repeat the same mistakes over and over before we begin to hear that still small voice suggesting that there is a truth encounter that we keep missing. We are so busy blaming others who do not seem to understand the importance of the issues, that we do not get it that perhaps something bigger than the issue is playing out. The cock crowing the third time is a life-changing event for all of us.

We need to look at how our behaviors are a denial of our Savior and an indicator of how desperately we need the healing and cleansing work of the

Holy Spirit. We cannot give away what we do not have. We try every day, and we try especially hard in ministry work. If we will be in the cleansing process with the Holy Spirit, we will find the healing that we require so that when invited to participate in a ministry, our motivation for being involved is from genuine love rather than neediness and selfishness.

Involvement in the sanctification process helps us meet and work with others from a place of humility and greater discernment. The Holy Spirit can do in us so much more that we can do on our own. This inner journey into which God is inviting us is a personal experience. I cannot give anyone my experience in this. I can only share my thoughts, ideas, information, and observations. The best that I can hope for is that a planted seed will spring into life in the hearts of all those in my sphere of influence...family, friends, clients, customers and myself.

Chapter 5

THE HOLY SPIRIT AND COMMUNICATION

This section seems to be essential. How do we allow the Holy Spirit to fill us with the fruit of the Spirit when we do not know how to communicate with Heaven or how Heaven communicates with us? As a matter of fact, it came as a surprise to me that God wanted to communicate with me. I had been taught intercessory prayer and prayers of supplication. I knew how to talk TO God, but I did not know how to talk WITH God. There were times when I heard from God as a response to prayers of intercession or supplication, but this is still different than talking WITH God.

"...ye have not, because ye ask not, Ye ask, and receive not, because ye ask amiss..."James 4:2,3. The Old and New Testaments are full of examples of God talking with His people. God's communion with Moses is so precious. It is like two Jewish fathers lamenting wayward children. Then there is the intimate time when God tucked Moses into the cleft of the rock so that Moses could see the essence of God...that something that could be described in terms of character traits. God's conversations with

Abraham are full of truths that offer us guidance today. There is much to be learned from Abraham's story.

We have an amazing account of conversation between God and Job. I am so grateful for Job's story for it gives us insight into the entire cosmic conflict. It helps us understand why we all have the "Job" experiences. God has always "come down" to His people. He modeled this in the sanctuary service, and in that service, He created a method of communicating with His people. God finds a way to communicate with each of us. For some, it may be in visions or little mental snapshots. For others, it may be in dreams. For others, it may be in the hearing of words. For others, it may be a "knowing".

The life and model of Jesus Christ is the greatest effort on God's part to communicate with His children. The Bible, an amazing transcript, has safely come down through ages and ages...this is a miracle in and of itself. If we are not sure how God speaks to us, we need to ask Him to show us.

Like most grandparents, I have amazing grandchildren. One day while visiting with an older grandchild, he asked me how you know if God is talking to you or if it is just your own mind. Isn't that an amazing thing for an eight year old to ask? Praise God! I suggested that we stop and pray about that. We asked God to let him know how He talks to him. We waited quietly for a little bit so that God could give him an answer. In a bit, I asked this sweet child what God had shared with him. He smiled and said that God showed him a picture of him drawing pictures. I asked him what he felt that God was telling him. With sparkling eyes and a big smile, he said, "I think that God speaks to me in pictures." Thank You, Lord!

It is in John 14:16 that Jesus tells the disciples about the Holy Spirit... the Comforter, the Spirit of truth. In Genesis 18:17 we have some amazing insight into God's desire to communicate with His people: *"And the Lord said, Shall I hide from Abraham that thing which I do,..."* God was planning to destroy Sodom and Gomorrah, and He wanted to share this information with Abraham. I want to be so connected with God that He will say, "Shall I hide from Linda this thing I am about to do?"

In Romans 8:26-27, we have some additional guidance: *"Likewise the Spirit also helpeth our infirmities: for we know not what we should pray for as we ought; but the Spirit itself maketh intercession for us with groanings which cannot be uttered. And he that searcheth the hearts knoweth what is the mind of the Spirit, because he maketh intercession for the saints according to the will of God."* The word "helpeth" has one particular meaning that I really enjoy. It is this idea: The Spirit picks us up and carries us over. That makes my heart happy! It reminds me of the groom carrying the bride across the threshold. We really do need help in getting from where we are to where we need to be....in the presence of God.

Not only do we need help with our positioning, but God knows what the subject of our prayers should be. This is such an acknowledgement that our motivations are selfish and self-centered, and it also tells us that we do not see the big picture. We are too invested in outcome to allow God to have His way. If we could see the end from the beginning, our prayers would be different. If we can trust the Trinity with the prayer process, then we will receive answers and guidance based on Their knowledge. This information is likely to challenge us. It is likely to "prove" us.

It gives me great peace to know that the Spirit intercedes for me. Sometimes I think I can feel His groaning within me as He translates my heart's desires into that which will match the will of God and bring about that which is in my highest and best good. The Spirit knows that my deepest longing is to be with God in all aspects of my life and living. He knows that part of me that yet needs healing and sanctification. He goes for that part.

In Zechariah 12:10, we have some beautiful words: *"And I will pour upon the house of David, and upon the inhabitants of Jerusalem, the Spirit of Grace and of Supplications: and they shall look upon me whom they have pierced, and they shall mourn for him, as one mourneth for his only son, and shall be in bitterness for him, as one that is in bitterness for his firstborn."* There is much that can be said about this scripture. For our study here, let us see the Spirit of grace and of supplications (prayer). The Holy Spirit intercedes for us. As we look upon the One who was pierced, we begin to see what it cost Heaven to rescue us.

Our prayers for forgiveness are made possible because He not only first loved us but also first made a pathway of forgiveness. It is the Holy Spirit's work to impress us with truth so that we are guided into all truth and understanding. Sometimes when I am reading about the life and death of Christ, the tears just fall. I mourn for there are no words. The Holy Spirit will use each prayer. These prayers have the potential for bringing about my own personal Gethsemane, Calvary, or resurrection. He may whisper to me: *"Linda, your name has come up. I know I can trust you with this. I love you and thank you for being willing to help me before the entire universe. Shall I hide from you that which I am about to do?"*

Chapter 6

THE FRUIT OF THE SPIRIT IS LOVE

"No one has greater love than this, that someone would lay down his life for his friends...you did not choose Me but I chose you." (**John 15:13**)

*G*od is love. Love is other-centeredness. For God so loved that He gave...His Son. When you get right down to defining love from this perspective, the way human's love and define love is very self-centered, self-serving.

We have the beautiful Biblical model of love and what it looks like and how it behaves. The fruit of the Spirit starts with love because God is love and everything is built on that. It even takes the Spirit's impartation of discernment to measure ourselves against this standard. It is a love that gave itself away. It risked everything...even Jesus becoming human gave up a part of Himself that He will never get back...He kept His scars after His resurrection. Does that not touch your heart at a very deep level?

God is love. We have to see this in all of scripture. Sometimes people want to make a difference between the "god" of the Old Testament and the Jesus of the New Testament. Jesus said that if we have seen Him, we have seen the Father. God is love. All the stories have to line up with this standard. If the Bible story seems not to line up with this, we need to ask for anointed eyes to see Him more clearly.

God is love. Not only must our perception of the Bible stories line up with this truth, I must line up all that I believe about God with this standard. God's identity has had a hatchet job done on it. Everywhere that Satan has had opportunity to malign God's character, he has done it. When we do not understand that God is love and put that truth into perspective for every day life, we not only do not see God as He is, we do not see ourselves as we are in Him. Man has created God in his own image.

The fruit of the Spirit begins with love because I must understand that I am loved. Once we get it that we are loved and that *"He delivers us because He delights in us"* (II Samuel 22:20) our relationship moves into a different place: I am a loved and lovable child of God. God rejoices over me! God said that He would be our God and we would be His people This is a covenant of relationship living with Him, and a covenant reality is that you must have others to put before yourself. He created us knowing that He would put us before Him. God is love. All things must be seen through this lens. 1John 4:8 doesn't say that God is loving (adjective). He is love (noun).

First Corinthians 13...love seeks not his own...it is all about relationship. Jesus modeled the relationship approach when He taught the disciples to pray, "Our Father..." The covenant relationship of love is always broken because of self-seeking. God steps in and offers us an amazing remedy. He is going to develop His character (the fruit of the Spirit) in us with the help of the Spirit. In this transformation process (sanctification), He will bring us step by step into the truth about Himself. God is love. As we are being changed by beholding Him, we learn the lies we believe about Him and the lies we believe about ourselves.

To really love is to give yourself. This kind of love is redemptive. It forces nothing. It forces no one. It is all based on choice. We cannot love anyone else until we understand that God loves us, and that kind of love gives us a model for learning: *"...but serve one another through love."* Galatians 5:13b. *"I appointed you that you should go out and produce fruit, and that your fruit remain so that whatever you ask the Father in My name, He will give you. This is what I command you: love one anothe. "John 15:16.*

In Galatians 5:6b it says, *"...what matters is faith working through love."* We love because He first loved us. Love is the foundation upon which my faith stands. Once my heart can get it that God's love is towards me, my faith in God is established, and I can rest from my own efforts.

When you look at the fruit of the Spirit, you can easily see that they are the extreme opposite of something that is negative. All of these extreme negatives have come as a consequence of the "spirit" of fear that took over Adam and Eve after the fall. These negatives are fear-based coping mechanisms. This is called sin, and ultimately sin is a breach in a relationship with God...like the prodigal son who was out of relationship with the father. He was still a son by virtue of the power of the blood relationship. His lack of relationship manifested in many inappropriate behaviors. These behaviors are an external manifestation of an internal spiritual state.

A "sin" (a behavior) may become "sin" (a state of being). God, through the work of the Holy Spirit, has given us a way to move out of the "state" of sin and into a putting away of sin (behaviors). The process of Him writing the law on our hearts and minds is an inside out work...changing my motivations and intentions as the Holy Spirit moves over the dark voids of my conscious and unconscious programming. *"When He the Spirit of truth is come, He will lead you into all truth" John 16:13.*

Christ, by His own blood, has purchased us. From a foundation of God's love to us, we have a platform for developing the ability to love ourselves and to love others. We need to receive before we can extend. As we grow in grace, we begin to realize that those external behaviors that are so unpleasant are really coping mechanisms for saints who are in need of emotional and spiritual healing.

Jehovah Rapha (the God who heals you) uses this cleansing process to get underneath the dysfunctional behaviors and find the faulty programming that is keeping us hostage to patterns of reacting that we know in our hearts are not truly Christian. That still, small voice is calling people to ask, "Where is my victory?" Praise God. This desire will have us turning toward God.

"By this shall all (men) know that you are my disciples, if you love one another (if you keep on showing love among yourselves). John 13:35 Amplified Bible

Chapter 7

THE FRUIT OF THE SPIRIT IS JOY

The first fruit is love, and God's love resulted in salvation. "Restore unto me the joy of Thy salvation." (Psalm 51:12)

It is not coincidental then that the second fruit is joy. Internalizing at the heart level that we are loved makes it possible to be joyful. It makes it possible for every other spiritual fruit to be developed within us.

"Ask, and ye shall receive, that your joy may be full." (John 16:24)

"That My joy might remain in you and that your joy might be full." (John 15:11)

God links asking and receiving with our joy being full. It is so much easier for me to ask and receive when I believe that I am loved. I see joy as courage, the "coming boldly before the throne of grace." Because I know that I am a child of God, I can have courage about asking. Psalm 16:8-11 has something interesting to say about joy: *"I have set the LORD always before me; Because He is at my right hand I shall not be moved. Therefore my heart is glad, and my glory rejoices; My flesh also will rest in hope. For You will not leave my soul in Sheol, Nor will You allow Your Holy One to see corruption. You will show me the path of life; In Your presence is fullness of joy; At Your right hand are pleasures forevermore."*

Because God is at our right hand:

- we shall not be moved
- our hearts are glad
- our glory (character) rejoices
- our flesh can rest in hope
- we do not need to be concerned about death and hell for He has overcome
- we have guidance for the path of life
- we have fullness of joy by being in His presence
- we have pleasures forever because we are positioned at His right hand.

As we look at the list above and follow its progression, we can see that joy is the consequence of being in His presence. Another way of saying this is that as we stay at the right hand of God, our experience will be one of being steadfast and glad. We will have a character change that shows on the outside. Our faith and trust will no longer struggle with the fears of this world. Daily we can rest. And, when the end of life comes, this rest that has already begun can continue as we know that He has gone before us and has overcome death and hell.

In His presence is FULLNESS of joy. Joy has everything to do with positioning...at the right hand of God. The right hand of God is always symbolic of favor. When we know that we are loved and have God's favor, the potential for experiencing all of the above is magnified. Wow, I want to live life from this perspective. I know that you do, too. Otherwise, you would not have picked up this book hoping that it would bless you in some way.

When I was younger, I looked for the checklist that would help me get with the program and get this business of being a Christian done correctly. If there is one thing that I have learned, it is this: About the time that I think I have it figured out, life happens. I find myself in one or more of those situations that contain the potential for grief, anger, shame, blame, despair, depression, and any of those other emotions and states of being into which we can fall. In tears, I ask God, "OK, what do I do with this? I thought I had it figured out this time, but here I am failing again. I know that You are faithful so it has to be my fault. What more do I need to understand?"

I was trying to get to the joy by "doing" things. Have you had your own checklists? Slowly, I have come to know that the only real joy to be had is His joy in me. This joy is not about never having tears or being confused. It is His joy that speaks to me in these times of distress saying, *"Peace be unto you: as my Father hath sent me, even so send I you. ...Reach hither thy finger, and behold my hands, and reach hither thy hand, and thrust it into my side: and be not faithless, but believing. ..blessed are they that have not seen, and yet have believed." John 20:21 – 29*

When God spoke the above words over me during a difficult time of life, I felt a joy and gratitude response in understanding that He, who had been crucified, could still say to me, "...blessed are they that have not seen, and yet have believed." Although I could not see past the present trial, He was saying, "Peace be unto you." When I asked to be excused from a painful experience, He said, *"I could not excuse my Son, and I cannot excuse my daughter. Linda, like Job, your name has come up. I trust you with this experience."*

53

His answer moved me from being Satan's victim to being a partner with God. Although the trial did not go away, my response to it changed dramatically. This does not mean that I enjoyed it. It does not mean that my tears stopped. Crucifixion hurts. What the Devil meant for my destruction, God used. New meaning came from the words: *"as my Father hath sent me, even so send I you."*

"Now the God of hope fill you with all joy and peace in believing, that ye may abound in hope, through the power of the Holy Ghost" Romans 15:13 When I look at this text, I stand amazed. My belief in this God of hope allows Him to fill me through the power of the Holy Ghost.

Life happens whether I am aligned with God or not. The rain falls on the just and the unjust. Alignment with God means that we are not alone when the storms come upon us. We have often heard it said that earth is not our home, we are just passing through. Hearing this is not the struggle. Believing it to the point that we stop trying to build a kingdom on earth is the greater challenge. Positioning at His right hand will keep us in the awareness that His favor is upon us as we "steward" that which is our part of this Earth School assignment.

When a child knows he/she has the favor of mom or dad, it just shows on those precious little faces. They reflect a joy that actually is coming from the heart of their parents. I want that! He has a place for us at His right hand. It is a place of favor. See again the little child that loves to sit next to mom or dad. They snuggle up. Or they share a book. Or they pat your hand. That is a picture of sitting at the right hand of God. He longs for us to love Him that way. Deep down, we also long to be loved that way.

As a student and teacher of natural health principles, I often see people who are trying to find their way out of fatigue, depression, anxiety, hopelessness, anger, and grief. Most often they are pursuing external solutions and chasing symptoms. They want to know what vitamin will "fix" this problem. As I visit with them and have an opportunity to educate them on how the body works, they begin to see the connection between the body, mind, emotions, and spirit. Yes, there are deficiencies that can lead to a lack of joy or hopelessness. The deficiencies occur because of missing nutrients in the diet and/or poor digestion and assimilation.

Most people are unaware that neuro-transmitters are actually made in the small intestines from the breakdown of protein in the diet. Protein deficiency and/or poor digestion which leads to poor assimilation will create these deficiencies. Correcting the gut and diet can be helpful in correcting this.

I have seen and heard of many people who have become involved in deliverance ministries and repeatedly need "deliverance" from the same thing. There is perhaps a physical dynamic that is being overlooked. I have worked with more than one person dealing with depression and self-abuse issues that cleared up when they removed gluten from their diets. Deficiencies, diet, and life-style habits can cause emotional problems, as can prescription drug contraindications.

I share these thoughts because it is important to honor the fact that we are more than just the physical. This awareness may be a matter of life and death for some people. Science is validating that as we think so are we. This brings us to another important dynamic that affects physical, emotional, and spiritual health: the lens through which we view life and our life experiences. If a child receives an inheritance of abuse, that child is probably going to view life through a lens of fear. All situations and relationships will be measured from that perspective. How does that person exchange the lens of fear and anxiety for a lens of faith and trust?

If you do a scripture search for the word joy, you will discover that it is often connected with being delivered from the enemy and/or with being in the presence of God or His work. This makes me very happy. As a person who experienced child abuse, I am so grateful that God opened the doors for me to find healing and release from that which was meant to destroy me.

In this respect, it is important that you stay at the right hand of God. I have seen so many people who are trying to get freedom from child abuse and other hurts become addicted to their processes. Their processes become their savior. Their work becomes their devotional experience. These are counterfeits.

Let us look again at these verses: *Ask, and ye shall receive, that your joy may be full" John 16:24. "That My joy might remain in you and that your joy might be full" John 15:11.* Joy is God's desire for us. Joy is an experience that is about being in relationship. If we have a subconscious programming (I am unworthy, I am undeserving, I am bad, etc.), there will be relationship difficulties with everyone including God.

It is my observation that God works gently with us. At one point, I felt very impressed that I had to stop being a people pleaser. It had become a place of idolatry in my life. In prayer, I felt very strongly that God was saying that unless I overcame in this area of my life, I would not be able to be obedient down the road. I would not be able to hear His voice as other voices were just too loud. As a "first-born fixer", this was really a hard message for me. We dress up this dysfunctional behavior in all kinds of Christian clothing. Never mind...it is what it is. A work of healing and victory was required.

Praise God! Now, I understand that staying at His right hand will mean that not everyone is going to be happy with me. Why was this so hard for me to understand? Why is it so hard for you to understand? Because we are raised believing that it is in some way our responsibility to keep others happy. How many times do we have to read the Bible stories before we see that God is always calling us to "come out of the father's house" so that we can become all that He has in mind for us. We can have no greater joy than to know that we are in His favor and positioned at His right hand.

As we study texts and perhaps see them in a fresh light, it is important to understand that I am putting Bible study together with physical processes that helps make the word of God flesh in our lives. As a child or teen you probably had some tricks that helped you learn or remember certain things. This physical process (music, singing, textured paper, eating M&Ms, etc.) helped make it a part of you. There are physical techniques for remembering scriptures and changing our programming from lie-based beliefs to scripture-based truth.

Think of the healings where Jesus engaged the physical and created healing...the hem of His garment, the mud on the eyes, washing in water, etc. If Jesus, who could have "spoken" healing, engaged the person by using physical processes, we should consider doing the same. These processes change everything because it embraces the totality of you—mind, body, spirit.

Love...when I know that I am loved
and that I am a loving and lovable child of God,
then I can have *joy*.

Chapter 8

THE FRUIT OF THE SPIRIT IS PEACE

"And the fruit of righteousness is sown in peace by those who make peace. James 4:18

"For the Kingdom of God is not meat and drink; but righteousness, and peace, and joy in the Holy Ghost. For he that in these things serveth Christ is acceptable to God, and approved of men. Let us therefore follow after the things which make for peace and things wherewith one may edify another" Romans 14:17.

The third fruit is peace. In Proverbs 12:20 we are told that those who promote peace have joy. Heaven has, through the cross of Christ, promoted cosmic peace. The Accuser has been silenced. The heavenly host has seen evil manifested to the point of killing the Son of God. And now, there is great joy over even one sinner that repents.

Now, you can now be at peace with yourself.

Now, you can now be at peace with others.

Someone once said that if we can get over ourselves, other people will not bother us. Those challenges to our peace that come from people, situations, or things are meant to help us see ourselves in a correct light. Our negative response to that with which we are at odds is a signal to us that we need to come up to a higher place. It is the invitation into the Spirit's cleansing process.

"Whom God hath set forth to be a propitiation through faith in his blood, to declare His righteousness for the remission of sins that are past, through the forbearance of God; to declare, I say, at this time His righteousness: that He might be just, and the justifier of him which believeth in Jesus" Romans 3:25-26.

The Spirit's peace includes the peace that is cosmic. It is the peace that Christ has accomplished as a result of the Cross of Calvary. The controversy has not been between God and man. The controversy has been between Heaven and the evil one. God was accused. Man had broken his relationship with God, and God could not be just if man was not made to pay the consequences which God Himself had pronounced....ye shall surely die. Yet God, through Christ, made a way. The peace is that Satan has been shown to be what he is...a liar and a murderer. Christ has the Divine right to give us what He intended from the beginning.

I believe that God has given us a wonderful visual aid in the story of the woman caught in adultery. She was set up and deceived by the evil ones who wanted to use her to trap Jesus. They brought her to Jesus, and threw her at His feet. They demanded that she be stoned for her sin. (John 8:5)

One day as I read this story again, I was amazed to see that her story is our story. The evil one set us up and deceived us. He wanted to trap God in his plan. He wanted to destroy us as the creation of God. He demanded our destruction. But God, through Jesus, made a way of escape for us. *"Now the God of peace, that brought again from the dead our Lord Jesus, that great shepherd of the sheep, through the blood of the everlasting covenant, make you perfect in every good work to do his will, working in you that which is well pleasing in his sight, through Jesus Christ; to whom be glory for ever and ever."* Hebrews 13:21. Do you see? When we begin to understand everything that God has done to (1) solve the cosmic dilemma and (2) restore the broken relationship with His people, it takes a great deal of pressure off.

He says that He has started the work, and He will finish the work. His bidding is His enabling, and all of His promises are given for our overcoming. Here is the work of the Holy Spirit making the word of God flesh in us as we are changed into the image of Christ. Seeking and participating in the work of grace upon our hearts is our only work. As the fruit of the Spirit manifest as a consequence of this work, we are changed from our character to His character.

Leaving off personal striving for perfection and allowing the Holy Spirit to do that work is a movement away from personal idolatry to worship of God. It is a movement from a man-centered approach of performance based religion to a God-centered approach that creates victory. Embracing these truths helps us develop peace with our own personal self. We are so often at odds with God and others because we are not at peace with ourselves. Likely, we are not even aware of this.

What we see in others that we would criticize is a signal that the same thing is working in us. It may not manifest in the same behavior, but we share the same level of pain as the person we would criticize. There is a story of six siblings that is an example of this dynamic...three boys and three girls, all of whom were abused as children. As they grew up in the shadow of this pain, the girls became perfectionists and the boys became involved in drugs, sex, and alcohol. It is so easy to criticize those involved in drugs, sex, and alcohol and applaud those who are addicted to perfectionism and to being church-aholics. Their behaviors are very different. The level of pain is the same.

How much lack of joy do we experience because we have not learned how to promote peace in our sphere of influence? When you know that you are loved, you have great joy. Knowing that you are loved and being filled with the joy of that salvation brings great peace. In Philippians 4:9 we are told: *"Those things, which ye have both learned, and received, and heard, and seen in me, do: and the God of peace shall be with you."* God's word is full of lists that offer us a way to see truth more clearly. These lists invite us to pay attention. Here we are being told to embrace what He has taught us, what He gave us, what we heard Him say. and what we saw Him do; and the result is that the God of peace shall be with you.

This scripture is another way of instructing us to come out of the father's and mother's house. We need to leave the people-pleasing practices and move to a place where God can re-create us in His image. One day in my prayer time, I had taken a troubling situation to Him in prayer. His answer: peace on earth, good will toward men. I have decided that since I no longer watch mystery movies...or any TV at all...that He is giving me the "mysteries" of the kingdom to search out and enjoy!

You remember that in Luke 2:14 we have the story of the birth of Christ and the angels saying: *"Glory to God in the highest, and on earth peace, good will toward men."* Keep in mind that my prayer was about a relationship issue. This seemed a strange answer to that. It just means that I have to think on it a little bit because the Lord wants to show me a bigger picture than just this one issue about which I prayed.

In this big picture, I had been struggling with how God creates a people who are in one accord. I do not observe that anywhere. And if it looks like it is there, just wait until someone does not get their way about something. I have tried to reconcile Matthew 7:6, cast not your pearls before swine and Matthew 10:14, shake the dust off your feet, with the idea of being in one accord. I could not do it. In both cases, this instruction was given in dealing with the "church" folks, but I am sure that it is applicable in any situation. God's word is like that.

One night in prayer I told God I just did not get it. He was going to have to give me some more instruction. I went to bed. As soon as I got into bed, Romans 14:17 came to mind. *For the kingdom of heaven is not meat and drink; but righteousness, peace, and joy in the Holy Spirit.* Immediately, I got up. I saw that it had application for my situation, and I put it together with Romans 3:22: *Even the righteousness of God which is by faith of Jesus Christ unto all and upon all them that believe; for there is no difference.* This may seem a strange combination, but bear with me.

It is important to know that translations say faith IN Jesus. This is incorrect. It is the righteousness OF God by faith OF Jesus. Big difference. Faith in Jesus is dependent upon me. God leaves nothing to chance. Note these thoughts:

- Righteousness is God's. Romans 3:22
- Peace comes from Jesus according to John 14:27: *Peace I leave with you, my peace I give unto you: not as the world giveth, give I unto you. Let not your heart be troubled or be afraid.*
- Joy is from the Holy Spirit. Romans 14:17

Well, what does that have to do with peace on earth, good will toward men? The issue is about peace. I could see that I was "earth." Yes, I was made of earth. Jesus came to earth (all of us...His creation from dust). At His coming, the angels pronounced peace. It covers all of us. Then the angels said "good will toward men." I saw that I have peace with Jesus, but that I do not have peace with men so I can have no good will to bring them. Without peace, I do not have the joy of the Holy Spirit.

62

I have been trying to find a way to have peace with men and come into unity. How do you "trust" people who hurt you. The issue is trust. What the Lord showed me was we do not have a Biblical example of that. In fact, we have an example of just the opposite. John 2:24-25: *But Jesus did not commit Himself unto them, for He knew what was in man, And needed not that any should testify of man; for He knew what was in man.* If Jesus did not trust men because He had a clear understanding of the untrustworthiness of man, I can do no better. I am not called to trust man. I am called to trust Jesus.

I must have my expectations in line with the reality that mankind is untrustworthy (all of us) because we are too invested in outcome and having our own way. He loved us while we were yet sinners. Another way of saying that is that He loved us even though we are untrustworthy. Once I saw the truth, I asked God to change my programming. What a relief I felt. This is why Jesus had been saying "Peace on Earth (me) good will to men". The only good will that we can bring to mankind is the realization that we are all untrustworthy...our expectations of each other need to be in line with that.

Otherwise, we keep expecting others to be where we are, to think like we think, to eat like we eat, to dress like we dress...all those external things by which we measure each other and the self. This is the only way we can be "of one accord". When we no longer hold each other accountable for being what we cannot be, when we correctly realize that we are all untrustworthy, then we can be of one accord. We cannot get to the "joy of the Holy Spirit" until we have this type of good will towards men. It is this type of good will that will allow someone to crucify you and you say, "Father, forgive them for they know not what they do."

Jesus did not need the approval or affirmation of others. He had the Father's approval, and He knew He was about the Father's business. We tend to be about our business and we want everyone's approval. This puts new light on the scriptures that tell us to cast not our pearls before swine and shake the dust off the feet and move on. As long as we are doing these things as a reaction to what has been done to us, it is still a wanting to control others. This is not good will towards men. When we leave off this state of fear or anger, and we have no escape or punishment agenda, then we can move on or cast not our pearls before swine. It is a matter of respecting what the other person wants.

It also adds greater understanding to 1 Peter 3:15 which says: *But sanctify the Lord God in your hearts; and be ready always to give an answer to every man that "asketh" you a reason of the hope that is in you, with meekness and fear (respect).* This is where we get into trouble...we do not wait to be asked. We try to give people our "news" when they have not given an indication that they want it. It is really our agenda that we are pushing all dressed up to be something else...maybe it is ministry, witnessing, teaching. If it is not wanted, then we take it personally.

In these situations, we need to ask ourselves: Why does this upset me? It is not about the other. It is about me. It is because we have an agenda or are invested in the outcome in some way. Our needs are not being met. We blame the other. People-pleasing and wanting people to please us is idolatry. It is a false god. As long as we have this idolatry going on, then we cannot get to the joy of the Holy Spirit.

Peace is what Jesus brought. It is a blessing pronounced over all of us. The way we keep this peace from living in us is that we are a house divided against ourselves. We will never have it as long as it is peace with man that we are endeavoring to find. Now, you may say, but what about all those scriptures that encourage us towards peace. Let us look at some of them.

In Mark 9:50 the scripture says to have peace with one another. This is the story of the man who was casting out demons in Jesus name and the disciples wanted Jesus to rebuke him. In verse 40 Jesus said that he that is not against us in for us. Let us look at the dynamics of this story. It is a great example of the dualistic mindset where we think it can only be one way. The disciples were thinking that they were the only ones who could cast out demons. They were right and anyone else was wrong. Jesus rebuked this. Oh that we would get this in our hearts and in our churches. The peace that the disciples were called to in this scripture was indeed a "good will towards men" type of peace.

In Hebrews 12:14 we are told to follow peace with all men, and holiness, without which no man shall see the Lord. In verse 15 it talks about the root of bitterness issue and how that must be addressed to have peace. It is telling us that our absence of peace is because of relationship issues and the resulting bitterness. Why? Because we expect our peace to come from men. In this verse Jesus has linked peace with all men with holiness... *without which no man shall see the Lord.* One of the meanings of holiness is agreement with God. To be in agreement with God is to know that the only "peace" available is the peace which Christ gives us. Peace comes from Jesus. Anything else is idolatry.

Now we have an interesting text in Matthew 10:34, where Jesus says: *"Think not that I am come to send peace on earth: I came not to send peace, but a sword."* This is a wonderful example where Jesus is trying to manage the expectations of the people. Like all of us, they were looking for "peace" in whatever way they defined it. It meant one thing to one person and another to someone else. He is saying here that although I bring peace on earth... peace of a cosmic nature...I came not to send peace, but a sword.

Do you get it? If you represent the truth on earth, you will be the "sword" that divides the truth from error. That does not make people happy. A sword divides. They crucified the Lord of peace because He did not bring peace in the way that they wanted it. There is such a huge lesson in this for us.

Peace is again mentioned in Romans 12:18 where it says *that if it be possible as much as lieth in you have peace with all men.* This whole chapter is about relationship issues. There is an ideal...that we treat others like we want to be treated, and there is the reality that we are selfish and untrustworthy people. This is obvious in that we would not have needed the guidance if it were not true.

I am glad that it says, *"if it be possible as much as lieth in you have peace with all men."* Sometimes the best peace you can have with someone is to stop expecting them to be what they cannot be (usually what we want them to be) and to stop expecting people to meet your needs. These expectations create a house divided against itself because it is always looking for an answer in others instead of Christ.

In John 20:21: *Then said Jesus to them again, Peace be unto you: as my Father hath sent me, even so send I you.* He gave them these words after His resurrection. The only peace that is real and that we have is that which our Lord gives us. He can still talk about peace even though He has been crucified by the untrustworthy people He came to save. This is the truth of the peace that we must have. Then we can have "good will towards men."

Peace is not non-disturbance. Peace is not sameness. I find that in some groups they talk of unity but it is not unity in diversity. It is unity in sameness. If you are not as they are, there will be no unity. There is only discomfort with the differences of others.

My prayer is that you will find Christ's peace in the middle of *"in this world you shall have trouble, but be of good cheer, I have overcome the world."* Let us continually look unto Him who is the author and finisher of our salvation. Peace comes from God. It is so important to put this truth in our hearts and minds. The world offers peace, peace, but there is no peace. I have seen people so medicated on drugs that were to bring them peace that they could not think, feel, or understand. Peace comes from God.

More guidance: *"And let the peace of God rule in your hearts, to the which also ye are called in one body; and be ye thankful"* Colossians 3:15. God's peace in our lives puts us in the position of being peaceful with others. When we understand that we no longer need to judge anyone or anything, it is amazing how much peace begins to flow. It is life-promoting energy.

We are told in Luke 6:37: *"Judge not, and ye shall not be judged: condemn not, and ye shall not be condemned: forgive, and ye shall be forgiven:"* I heard one teacher say, "If you spot it, you've got it." We might laugh at the humor in this, however, it comes back to teach us in those moments when we find something to criticize, judge, and condemn in others. It is an invitation into God's training school. It is an invitation into cleansing. It is an invitation to follow Him.

More guidance: *"And the very God of peace sanctify you wholly; and I pray God your whole spirit and soul and body be preserved blameless unto the coming of our Lord Jesus Christ"* 1 Thessalonians 5:23.

The word sanctify means:

- to set apart to a sacred purpose or to religious use
- to free from sin: purify
- to impart or impute sacredness, inviolability, or respect
- to give moral or social sanction to make productive of holiness of piety (observe the day of the Sabbath, to sanctify it Deuteronomy 5:12.)

This is beautiful news for us! God has set us apart for a sacred purpose; freeing us from the broken relationship, while both imparting and imputing Heaven's blessing of the Son of God upon us so that we are made productive of holiness. Wow! People are pursuing so many things today to find peace. Most of it is about the externals of life. Some of it is about emptying one's mind. Romans 12:2 tells us: *"And be not conformed to this world: but be ye transformed by the renewing of your mind, that ye may prove what is that good, and acceptable, and perfect, will of God."*

One of the great tragedies of the time in which we live is that the mind, body, spirit connection has been fragmented into special fields. Each field sees your problem from their own perspective. I recently had a client come to me. She had been doing counseling, and she was still depressed and tired. When I checked her, she needed some very specific nutrition that would encourage the production of serotonin. When I read her the description of how a person feels with this deficiency, she got tears in her eyes. It was such good news to know that the struggle was not mental, emotional, or situational...it was nutritional.

In the 1 Thessalonians 5:23 quote above, God's prayer is that our whole spirit, soul, and body be preserved blameless. God's prayer for us in John 17 is that we will be one with the Godhead. Oneness is very important to God. How can His peace be in us if our spirit, soul, and body has been fragmented? It is like trying to serve more than one master. Romans 6:16 says it this way: *"Do you not know that to whom you s yourself slaves to obey, you are that one's slave whom you obey, whether of sin leading to death or of obedience leading to righteousness."* See also 2 Peter 2:19 where Peter speaks of false teachers.

Like love and joy, peace is from God. It is not an external that comes from the ways of men. It is a living experience that will even defy logic. It is a state of being that will energize everything we do and touch everyone with whom we come in contact. It is a prerequisite for the next fruit...patience.

Love...when I know that I am loved
and that I am a loving and lovable child of God,
then I can have *joy.*

When I have joy (in God and in myself),
I am satisfied and trust God with everyone and everything.
I have *peace.*

Chapter 9

THE FRUIT OF THE SPIRIT IS PATIENCE

The fourth fruit is patience. Isn't that amazing? You see, you cannot have patience, until you have peace. It is the Spirit's work in us that allows us to look at people and/or situations and say: "I'm peaceful with allowing God to work this out." When we begin to demand and force things to go our way, we lose our peace and impatience surfaces. *"By your patience possess your soul." (Luke 21:19).*

The Holy Spirit is always ready to help us. When we lose our peace and become impatient, He will say: "Think about it, why does this matter to you? This has become a place that shows your spiritual immaturity. Let's work through this and come up to a higher place." Oh, you mean, my impatience is "my" problem, not someone else's fault? Yeah!

When we demand that things be the way we want them to be, we are actually saying that we do not trust God with our lives. When we blame our lack of patience on something or someone else, we are creating a false god. When we refuse to be "disturbed," we are fighting against Heaven. *"My brethren, count it all joy when you fall into various trials, knowing that the testing of our faith produces patience. But let patience have its perfect work, that you may be perfect and complete, lacking nothing" James 1:2-4.*

It is misplaced expectations that get us into trouble. We expect people and things to do what we think they should do. I expect the computer to work, and when it does not, I am not happy. Why do I expect perfection from that which is not? Why do I expect to never have any challenges that force me to develop character?

A favorite writer of mine, Oswald Chambers, says that we need to understand that when we face trials they are not our trials but the trials to the Christ within us. And when we have victories, they are not our victories, but the victories of the Christ within us. Is that not wonderful?! I do not even need to take these trials personally. It is just the devil's way of getting back at God!

A supreme example of peace is Christ. He had peace because He was in unity or agreement with His Father. His peace was not controlled by His external life. His external life had power for good because He was aligned with Heaven. Obviously, this did not mean that He was free of trials or suffering. His peace gave Him amazing patience. This patience allowed Him to see things as they really were. He took nothing personally...even man's betrayal.

The Lord's model comes from John 2:23 – 25. Jesus had His expectations of men in line with reality: *"for He knew what was in man."* Isn't it amazing that He knew what was in man, and, yet, He loved us enough to die for us? Getting our expectations in line with reality is a place of personal freedom. We can quit demanding that everyone else be what we want/need them to be. The truth is that no one was put on this planet to make me happy. That is my work with the Godhead.

While having all the power that is possible to have, Jesus never forced anything. We are so much about "forcing" our way. We lose our patience and kick into control mode. Control is not peaceful or patient. Christ had peace and was patient when everything "seemed" out of control. He knew that the storms were just an illusion. If we, as John the Revelator did, could see behind the veil, we would see God high and lifted up...and in control.

A great opportunity exists in that which challenges our peace and, therefore, our patience. There are lessons to be learned or unlearned. One of those lessons in peace is that we are able to align ourselves with this truth: We do not need to expect that our experience will be less difficult than that of our Lord. God did not excuse His own Son, and He doesn't excuse His adopted children. There is a great deal of peace that comes when we align our expectations with reality. With that peace, comes patience with what "seems" to be a challenge.

In Romans 5:3-5 (Holman Bible), we find this counsel: "*...we rejoice in our affliction because we know that affliction produces endurance, endurance produces proven character, and proven character produces hope. This hope does not disappoint, because God's love has been poured out in our hearts through the Holy Spirit who was given to us.*"

Patience is defined as cheerful or hopeful endurance and long-suffering. In the above texts we see this progression: affliction → endurance → character → hope. This process is God's work in us through the trials we have, the relationship issues we have...situations and people. In the beginning we chose to "know" good and evil. This process is about learning to "discern" between good and evil and choose the good. The hope that develops through this process is a hope that does not disappoint because it is based in God's love being in our hearts. It is an inside out change. What a comforting thought that on the other end of affliction is hope...hope that does not disappoint. What Adam and Eve chose has been a grand disappointment. God's redemptive process never disappoints.

Again, using the Holman Bible, James 1:3, 4 adds some additional insight regarding the trials. "*Knowing that the testing of your faith produces endurance. But endurance must do its complete work so that you may be mature and complete, lacking nothing."* It is faith that is being tested. Does God not know if we have faith or not? Yes, He knows, but remember the Accuser has to be shown. We chose this when we chose not to trust God. You might say that now God is being held captive by our choices. We could contemplate that for a while.

Testing creates endurance. Our developing endurance creates a mature and complete character...lacking nothing. James 5:10-11 points us to Job's experience and to consider the outcome "from the Lord." During my trials, it has helped me to look forward to the outcome and trust that it is from the Lord, and He never lets me down. My Cup of Tea study, Job's Story—Moving From Fear-based to Faith-based Living, looks at this in much more detail.

At one point, I was doing some emotional clearing work around impatience. My daughter said that she was surprised at that because she felt that I was the most patient person that she knew. I laughed and said that I was pretty patient with everyone else, but I was very impatient with myself. Every time I got impatient with myself, I took it as a Divine appointment with God to come up to a higher place in my relationship with myself.

I am the work of His hands. I deserve some kindness and compassion. It was really eye-opening, and the Lord showed me many wounds from childhood. My impatience with myself was self-punishment for my imperfections. With the Lord's healing, I am much happier. As I see the truth about who I am in Christ, these wounding lies are cleansed from my soul temple. Thank you, Lord!

Using the Holman Bible, Colossians 1:11-12 says: *"May you be strengthened with all power, according to His glorious might, for all endurance and patience, with joy giving thanks to the Father who has enabled you to share in the saint's inheritance in the light."* He enables us. Because His bidding is His enabling, the Divine working through the human, is a witness to not only what God can do, but it forever silences the Accuser. We get to share in the saint's inheritance, and the Accuser cannot raise an objection.

In 2 Thessalonians 3:5 (Holman Bible) we are encouraged: "*May the Lord direct your hearts to God's love and Christ's endurance.*" This is beautiful...our endurance comes from Christ. He endured unto death. This endurance is available to us. Its purpose is our purifying. It is about our cleansing, our character development...our completeness is His fruit of the Spirit coming to maturity in us. Praise God!

Love...when I know that I am loved
and that I am a loving and lovable child of God,
then I can have *joy*.

When I have joy (in God and in myself),
I am satisfied and trust God with everyone and everything.
I have *peace*.

When my expectations are in line with reality
and I trust God with my own process
and that of other people,
I have *patience*.

Chapter 10

THE FRUIT OF THE SPIRIT IS KINDNESS

The next fruit is kindness. When our peace remains and patience follows peace, then kindness that is real and honest can manifest. In this growth process, if we find that it is easier to be kind to some folks and harder to be kind to others, then we are again being invited to come up to a higher place. Why am I being a respecter of persons when God is not? Whatever I dislike about someone is a mirror to something within myself. It is the mote and beam concept from the Bible: If you spot it, you've got it. So, again, our propensity to be unkind to someone is showing us something about ourselves. That other person is just being used by God to train me. I can actually thank God for that other person and then ask the Holy Spirit to cleanse me and show me what lie I believe that makes me think that I can justify this type of behavior.

People often want to be kind because they believe that it will come back to them. We often teach children the concept that "kindness comes back." What we need to be careful of, however, is making kindness another type of business transaction. If our kindness is based on the potential of a return of some sort, then it has become a transaction that is sure to disappoint us. We can dress this up in all kinds of spiritual garb, it is still just business.

There is a huge difference between civility, the secular version of kindness, and the Spirit's fruit of kindness. Civility is impersonal. I have seen people be so civil that it was very obvious that they were being unkind. This lack of kindness can then be charged to the offended person's lack of appreciation for the civility extended to them. This may be another type of business transaction called payback. David showed Jonathan's son kindness out of a love and respect for Jonathan. He had no obligation to be kind, and there was nothing to gain from it. It was a kindness that emphasized again that David would not raise his hand against the Lord's anointed or Saul's household.

There are some forms of kindness that may not feel good, but accomplishes much good for us. This is the kindness that confronts. In Psalm 141:5 we read: *Let the righteous smite me; it shall be a kindness: and let him reprove me; it shall be an excellent oil, which shall not break my head:...*" The secret to success in this, however, is to be on God's timetable and not our own. This story is a perfect example of the delicacy of this type of kindness.

There were two women who met regularly for intercessory prayer for others. One day, one of them felt impressed that the other one had a serious situation developing about which much prayer was needed. Asking God what to do with what she was told, He told her to keep it to herself until the correct time. In the meantime, she was to pray about the situation. These women continued to meet together regularly. All the while, the keeper of the information was waiting to be told when to speak. A year later, the subject came up, and she was able to speak what she knew to the other lady.

By this time, the lady was ready to receive truth. The lady asked her how long she had known this, and she was told that God had spoken this information one year before. She was overwhelmed with God's love and mercy in putting someone in her life to pray "silently" for an entire year about something that was pretty messy. This type of kindness is under the control of the Holy Spirit. We cannot take an ounce of credit for it.

As I looked for Biblical examples of the word "kindness," I came across "brotherly kindness" in 2 Peter 1. Wow! This is an amazing study. Again, we will find God giving us a list. Perhaps it would be well to spend a little time in these verses. We will come up with some beautiful gems of truth, and our study of kindness will also be enhanced.

Verse 1: *"Simon Peter, a servant and an apostle of Jesus Christ, to them that have obtained like precious faith with us through the righteousness of God and our Savior Jesus Christ:"*

Let us establish that their faith was through the righteousness of God and the Savior Jesus Christ. This is very important. The righteousness that I get to claim is NOT my righteousness. I have no righteousness...end of story. My faith, the substance of something not seen, the evidence of something hoped for, finds its foothold in the faith that was Christ's. The righteousness that covers me is Christ's. I have no righteousness. I can have no faith except the faith that Christ imparts to me from His own storehouse. It is the faith of Jesus that created a Savior. He allows me to use His faith. How totally amazing.

When God established His sanctuary in the wilderness for the children of Israel, He was allowing them to practice the promise of Christ. This was a visual aid for the substance of something not seen, the evidence of something hoped for...the work of Christ. Every aspect of the sanctuary service was about God pursuing His people. It is Heaven's rescue of planet earth. Now, as we humans tend to do, we take God's initiative and turn it into a work of our own hands. We seem bent on finding a way to take credit for His work. And this is what happened with the sanctuary system. By the time that Christ came, it had become a works orientation that did nothing to prepare the way for the Messiah. It was a system that would actually crucify the Messiah. There is such a huge message in this for us today. Father, open our eyes.

Verse 2: *"Grace and peace be multiplied unto you through the knowledge of God, and of Jesus our Lord."* Grace and peace are possible because this "knowledge" (precious faith through the righteousness of God and our Savior Jesus Christ) is a huge relief. This is why it is called the good news. Let us partner this with Jude 1 and 2: *"Jude the servant of Jesus Christ and brother of James, to them that are sanctified by God the Father, and preserved in Jesus Christ, and called: Mercy unto you and peace, and love, be multiplied."*

- Sanctified by God the Father
- Preserved in Jesus Christ
- Called

Yes! Mercy, peace and love have been multiplied to us and continue to be multiplied to us. Praise God!

Verse 3: *"According as His divine power hath given unto us all things that pertain unto life and godliness, through the knowledge of Him that hath called us to glory and virtue."* These words just blow me away! His divine power has given us everything that pertains to life and godliness THROUGH the knowledge of Him. Am I beholding God regularly? Am I gaining a knowledge of Him that is not only theological and intellectual, but is also experiential? Do I know Him in the intimate "oneness" relationship that He desires for us to have?

He has called us to:

Glory—what does this mean? In John 17:4, Jesus says: *"I have glorified thee on the earth; I have finished the work which thou gavest me to do."* Glory has something to do with finishing the work that God has appointed us to do. Look at Hebrews 2:7: *"Thou madest him a little lower than the angels; thou crowned him with glory and honor, and didst set him over the works of thy hands: Thou has put all things in subjection under his feet. For in that he put all in subjection under him, he left nothing that is not put under him."*

Glory and honor are connected with being who we were created to be, doing what we were created to do, and finishing the work that has been ours to do. These words so touch my spirit and call me into a higher place in my understanding of my purpose on the planet.

Virtue—what does this mean? In Strong's Concordance, the Greek for virtue (#703) means manliness (valor), excellence, praise...taken from #730 which means male (as stronger for lifting), male, men. Now, I am female. These words really touch my heart; especially "as stronger for lifting." We are called into a relationship with someone who has valor and excellence. We are called into a relationship with someone who can do something that I cannot do: He is stronger for lifting. He lifts me. He lifts you. He lifts sin off of us and places it on Himself.

Verse 4: *"Whereby are given unto us exceeding great and precious promises; that by these ye might be partakers of the divine nature, having escaped the corruption that is in the world through lust."* There is so much power in this verse that has not been understood and engaged.

In Psalm 119:11: *"Thy word have I hid in mine heart, that I might not sin against thee."* In John 17:17: *"Sanctify them through thy truth, thy word is truth."* In John 8:32: "And ye shall know the truth, and the truth shall make you free." God's word has the potential of becoming flesh in us. The promises of God have the potential of making us partakers of the divine nature. The promises of God help us escape the corruption that is in the world. I see this as a creation experience. The Spirit is hovering over the dark and void places of our lives. He waits for God to speak. God speaks. Then the Spirit brings light that dispels the darkness and guides us into all truth. This can only happen if we are in the word. Our minds must be reprogrammed with the word of God.

Verses 5 – 7 *"...add to your faith virtue; and to virtue knowledge; and to knowledge temperance; and to temperance patience; and to patience godliness, and to godliness brotherly kindness; and to brotherly kindness charity."*

Our faith is in the righteousness of God manifested in the work of Christ. Christ is the virtuous One. Knowledge must have a platform. That platform is God's righteousness and the work of Christ. This foundation makes it possible for the Spirit to fulfill in us the rest of the verse:

Temperance/stewardship: be temperate in your own estimation of self. Being a steward of knowledge carries with it a responsibility of patience. We must be patient with self, God, and others.

Patience embraces the truth that God is at work in all of us. Patience accepts that we are not all at the same place in our understanding. This is so huge in developing a Godly disposition about what we may perceive as the shortcomings in the church and its members. When we have patience (trust that God is at work in all), then our eyes can be taken off man and placed upon God and His word and work. Godliness is devotion to God. We must have this grounding. Otherwise, we will be devoted more to self's agenda and/or the agendas of others.

Brotherly kindness is a consequence of a relationship with God. It is a natural extension of that love for God. It is the external manifestation of an internal state of being called charity. Charity is what happens within us as we allow the Holy Spirit to work out: *"He must increase, but I must decrease"* John 3:30. It is only through the Spirit's work that a greater degree of self sacrifice or renunciation becomes possible. It is God's manifestation in a "temple" that is dedicated to bringing glory to His name.

Well, Second Peter was a bit of a detour, but the scene was worth the time! As I study these things, there are moments when it flashes through my mind that God is giving us the mysteries of His kingdom. In the garden, we settled for being as gods knowing good and evil. Are you tired yet of knowing the evil? I am. What we need is to be able to DISCERN between good and evil and choose good. What God is giving us here is how we can come back to His original intent...being in His image and one with the Godhead. Kindness and brotherly kindness also implies that I have embraced the truth that we are all brothers and sisters. God's kindness toward us changes us so that our kindness towards others allows a healing stream from Heaven to continue to flow.

Love...when I know that I am loved
and that I am a loving and lovable child of God,
then I can have *joy.*

When I have joy (in God and in myself),
I am satisfied and trust God with everyone and everything.
I have *peace.*

When my expectations are in line with reality
and I trust God with my own process and that of other people,
I have *patience.*

When my peace remains and patience follows peace,
then ***Kindness*** that is real and honest can manifest.

Chapter 11

THE FRUIT OF THE SPIRIT IS GOODNESS

This next text blows me away!

*"When He shall come to be glorified in His saints, and to be admired in all them that believe because our testimony among you was believed in that day. Wherefore also we pray always for you, that our God would count you worthy of this calling, and fulfill all the good pleasure of **His goodness**, and the work of faith with power: That the name of our Lord Jesus Christ may be glorified in you, and ye in Him, according to the grace of our God and the Lord Jesus Christ."*
2 Thessalonians 1:10-12

Jknow that this text is talking about the visible return of Christ, however, allow me some creative liberty...***When He shall become glorified in His saints and be admired in them...***

Do you want to have God glorified in you? Do you want all Heaven and earth to admire God because of you? Doesn't that just go right to your heart? And God counts us worthy of this calling! God help us measure ourselves as does Heaven. He seeks to fulfill all the good pleasure of His goodness...through the work of faith with POWER. This power is the Holy Spirit's work of infilling us with the fruit of the spirit which is a reflection of the character of God (see Exodus 33:19 and 34:6 and 7).

It is interesting that when you look up the word goodness in the Bible that it is used to mean what God does as well as a characteristic of His nature. Goodness (agathosune) denotes an active, even aggressive, goodness, more than an excellence of character, it is character energized, expressing itself in good deeds. Let us bullet point God's good deeds toward us:

- God glorified in His saints
- God admired in His saints
- God counts us worthy of this calling
- God fulfils all the good pleasure of His goodness
- God fulfils the work of faith with power
- The name of Jesus may be glorified in us
- And that we are glorified in Him
- According to the grace of God and Jesus Christ

This type of goodness is of Heaven. We cannot take credit for it. It is Spirit living out in us God's will. It is Spirit showing the universe what God can do in a willing vessel. It is Spirit vindicating God to the universe, and we are chosen to participate. How incredibly awesome is God's goodness and God's amazing grace! The "goodness" of God often refers to His gracious generosity of providing for our needs. *Psalms 23: surely goodness and mercy shall follow me all the days of my life: and I will dwell in the house of the Lord forever.*

In a study of the fruit of the Spirit, it is easy to forget that it is God's "fruit" that is growing in us. It is not our own. We really do not have any. The Bible gives us visual aids that show what goodness looks like in action.

When God created everything, He pronounced it good. I believe that there is a real spiritual lesson for us in the example that God pronounced "good" over all the works of His hand. We are that, too!

Because of this, I would say that God's original intent for us is "good." Again, the fruit is not, first of all, something we do. It is something we become as God redeems us from the ways of this world. It is wonderful that this goodness is God's! When manifesting in us, we will see all sorts of good works and kind deeds. Greater than that, however, is that we are His goodness manifesting upon the earth. This puts a different perspective on it because we cannot take credit for it, and we will be very aware of that.

Sometimes God's goodness would have us NOT do anything. Now, that will be uncomfortable for all us "doers" in the crowd. Sometimes God's goodness will have us be silent when our humanity is wanting to scream in defense of something. Only God's goodness will know when to engage or not. I have even seen God's goodness tell someone NOT to pray for a person. This can make us very uncomfortable.

God's goodness is always trying to get us back to His original intent in our creation...we are one with Him. Our efforts toward goodness are generally some form of us buying something from others: validation, respect, power, prestige, honor, etc. It was God's goodness that finally brought an end to the Ammonite nation because they were unredeemable. God no longer allowed them to be a source of evil. This type of "goodness" is sometimes difficult for us to understand.

Have you ever had a situation where you repeatedly did good, but the effect was that those involved never assumed responsibility for their actions. They just became more needy and less accountable. Finally, you saw that you were doing nothing good in allowing this. We do not know on the front end that this will be the story. It does not feel so good to us when it is happening.

God always knows at the start what will happen. His goodness allows even evil to fully mature. No one can say that they did not have enough chances. Justice gives a man what he deserves. Goodness tries to give a man what will be helpful for spiritual growth and maturity. It offers people chance after chance. Overcome evil with good (Romans 12:21), I think that maybe this is the purpose of God's goodness. The human way is to name things that we do not understand as dumb, stupid, or evil. Then we set out to overcome that with force...gossip, war, evil surmising, hostility, and all those other things that can be dressed up in religious garb.

The power of God in His goodness waits. Even in the cleansing of the temple, the unrighteous fled from His presence because of the power of His goodness emanating from Him. This is a type of judgment scene. The power of the Man with the whip was not physical. They knew they had been weighed in the balance and found wanting. What fellowship does light have with darkness? None. His goodness is revealed in the temple cleansing scene. It was their awareness of their sins that could have been a wake up call to repentance. God was still waiting even though they had fled the building.

God's goodness steps into man's life and waits. For instance, the man at the pool of Bethesda...God waited when He asked him if he wanted to be whole. When He told him to take up his bed and walk, He waited until the man decided to do it. The man could have decided not to walk. How is God's goodness stepping into our lives, in our temples, and our pools? He is waiting. We are often uncomfortable in the waiting process. It disturbs us. It feels out of control. In all this, God's goodness is being manifested, and He is instructing us regarding His processes.

I think that there is something at work in this fruit of the Spirit being before the next one...faithfulness. Learning from both sides of goodness, we are prepared for the development of faithfulness.

Love...when I know that I am loved
and that I am a loving and lovable child of God,
then I can have *joy.*

When I have joy (in God and in myself),
I am satisfied and trust God with everyone and everything.
I have *peace.*

When my expectations are in line with reality
and I trust God with my own process and that of other people,
I have *patience.*

When Christ's peace remains in me, and patience follows peace,
then *Kindness* that is real and honest can manifest.

Chapter 12

THE FRUIT OF THE SPIRIT IS FAITHFULNESS

In Luke 12:42, faithfulness is linked with being a steward. Faithfulness is a relationship dynamic. Look at verse 42 in the context of the entire chapter as it involves the faithfulness principle of "where your treasure is, there will your heart be also." See verse 34. Faithfulness includes what you do with your life and body—inside and out. It includes a faith and trust response regarding those things in life that have the potential for anxiety and worry...verse 22: *"Take no thought for your life, what ye shall eat; neither for the body what ye shall put on."*

Faithfulness embraces the truth that the "Father knows you have need of these things." Do I believe this? In the context of Luke 12, faithfulness includes observing the signs of the times and being prepared for the Master's return. There is so much that could be said here. Some people just sit down, do nothing, and wait. This is not faithfulness. Others get so caught up with the doing that they forget that they are stewards and not the Master.

Faithfulness includes being stewards over that which the Master has placed in our hands, realizing that it is not ours, but His. Faithful stewards will seek first that which supports the Master...the kingdom of God. The

Master will then provide everything else. This faithfulness implies that the Master can be trusted. Do we live our lives as if this is true for us?

In the context of Luke 12, faithfulness includes understanding that there is no peace on this earth. There will be divisions among people. Partner Matthew 5 (the Beatitudes) with Luke 12 and there is a greater understanding of these issues. Faithfulness includes dealing correctly with relationship issues, and understanding that each day has the potential for Gethsemane, Calvary, and resurrection.

Christ, in speaking the Beatitudes, was sweeping away the lies that were keeping the people in bondage. They believed lies about themselves, about God, about others, about the church, and church leadership. They had been taught a man-centered performance based theology. Christ was sweeping all the lies away. He was bringing them truth that would set them free. He brought the kingdom of Heaven down to them in His words. His words in the Beatitudes acknowledged where they were in their real life situations.

He was managing their expectations of what the real kingdom of Heaven is about. His words gave them similar guidance that the laws of Moses gave the children of Israel...how to live in relationship with God and man. While faithfulness can be observed through the things we do, the motivation for faithfulness comes from who we are in the relationship with the Master. The truly faithful steward knows and respects the relationship between himself and the Master. He recognizes that the Master needs him. This is beautiful. And he knows that he needs the Master.

Faithfulness includes the acceptance of gifts, talents, prosperity, and responsibility with a steward's heart and understanding. Faithfulness engages the truth of: he that is faithful over little will be faithful over much. Faithfulness looks forward to the Master's return and to continuing to serve in even larger capacities as the Master has need. In the context of Luke 12, faithfulness embraces the experiences of a lifetime. This is an important idea. The fruit of the Spirit build on each other. That is not to say that the Spirit is limited in His work, however, there is a cosmic law of choice and consequence that even God obeys.

I suggest that without the development of those previous fruit of the Spirit, it may be hard to be faithful...especially as we wait for the Master's return. The delay has been long. Luke 12 also talks about the delay. I think that the Master would have liked to come before now, but for some reason He has experienced a delay. Some writers suggest that He is waiting on us. The wheat and tares grow together until harvest...for they are known by their fruit. He is waiting for the fruit to develop.

The following words amaze me. In these few verses, we are given a crash course on the sanctuary process which is a description of the work of being filled with the fruit of the Holy Spirit.

> "...I will put my laws into their hearts, and in their minds will I write them; And their sins and iniquities will I remember no more. Now where remission of these is, there is no more offering for sin. Having therefore, brethren, boldness to enter into the holiest by the blood of Jesus, by a new and living way, which he hath consecrated for us, through the veil, that is to say, his flesh, and having an high priest over the house of God; let us draw near with a true heart in full assurance of faith, having our hearts sprinkled from an evil conscience, and our bodies washed with pure water. Let us hold fast the profession of our faith without wavering; for he is faithful that promised;..." Hebrews 10:16-22.

The cleansing process is the work of the Most Holy Place...beyond the veil. In that apartment, God writes the law on our hearts and minds (law is in the ark of the covenant, and it is in the Most Holy Place). Our relationship as stewards includes being faithful as individual priests and as a community of priests. Our High Priest has a work to do with us in His sanctuary process. Most of us have embraced the courtyard's cross and blood. We need to enter into the Holy Place process of beholding the Lamb of God, and into the Most Holy Place process of hearing from God as He directs the development of the fruit of the Spirit which is the process of sanctification.

Heaven is faithful in its work of developing the fruit of the Holy Spirit in us. Our free will, however, is never violated. We must choose daily to be "faithful" to a partnership with God that allows this work to continue. The delay in His coming is not only a challenge, it is an opportunity to come more completely under Heaven's covering of truth and life. As we manage the delay of Christ's return, another visual from the Bible can be helpful. Jesus is the vine and we are the branches. If we do not stay attached, we will not be nourished. This is the abiding process. This is sanctification. Be faithful as a steward of this relationship.

Love...when I know that I am loved
and that I am a loving and lovable child of God,
then I can have *joy.*

When I have joy (in God and in myself),
I am satisfied and trust God with everyone and everything.
I have *peace.*

When my expectations are in line with reality
and I trust God with my own process and that of other people,
I have *patience.*

When Christ's peace remains in me, and patience follows peace,
then *kindness* that is real and honest can manifest.

When kindness is not outcome driven, when Christ is my heart's desire,
I will be a *faithful steward* of what is important to Him.

89

Chapter 13

THE FRUIT OF THE SPIRIT IS MEEKNESS

2 Corinthians 10:1: "Now I Paul myself beseech you by the meekness and gentleness of Christ, who in presence am base among you, but being absent am bold toward you."

As with all of the fruit of the spirit, we must understand that these fruit are OF Christ. This is such good news for we can get a bit down as we realize just how far from the mark we can fall on a daily basis. God is so amazing in that He can take our failures and use them as a mirror so that we can see our need of His divine intervention. Like the hammered brass on the laver that reflected a broken image of those who stood at its cleansing fount, so our failures can help us reach out for cleansing through the washing of water by the word (Ephesians 5:26).

The meekness of Christ being manifested in us makes it possible to fulfill *Matthew 3:15: "But sanctify the Lord God in your hearts: and be ready always to give an answer to every man that asketh you a reason of the hope that is in you, with meekness and fear."* This is an amazing text. Do you notice that we are to give an answer to those who ask. Isn't this where we get into trouble? You see, when we start giving answers to those who have not asked, it is because we are lacking in meekness. We have moved from being used by the Spirit to using the Word for something other than it is intended.

Give an answer to those that ask you for a reason for you hope...and do it with meekness and fear. I would translate fear as respect and honor. The meekness of Christ recognizes divine appointments. The meekness of Christ understands that when someone is comfortable enough with you to ask you a question regarding spiritual things, they deserve a respectful response. The meekness of Christ in you guarantees that the Spirit will give you the words that are correct for any situation.

I love how Paul speaks of himself: *"who in presence am base among you, but being absent am bold toward you."* This is the meekness of Christ manifesting Paul's opinion of himself. His words offer us some additional guidance. Sometimes it is easier to be absent and send a letter so you can evaluate your words before they are mailed. In the face-to-face encounters, we definitely need to remember that we are "base" and it is the meekness of Christ that must respond to questions.

Another example of the meekness of Christ is in James 3:13: *"Who is a wise man and endued with knowledge among you? Let him show out of a good conversation his works with meekness of wisdom."* This text reminds us that we may be blessed with knowledge, but be critical and overbearing people. Knowledge is information. Wisdom makes application of information, and meekness of wisdom allows the Holy Spirit to express wisdom at the appropriate time.

Meekness is not only about how we deal with others, but it is also about how we receive from others and God. An example of this is in James 1:21: *"Wherefore lay apart all filthiness and superfluity of naughtiness, and receive with meekness the engrafted word, which is able to save your souls."* We all have need of laying aside naughtiness. We must receive with meekness the word that can save us. Truth presented without meekness is likely to create defensiveness. The meekness of Christ is needed in the one presenting truth and in the one receiving truth.

Another example of this is found in 2 Timothy 2: 24, 25: *"And the servant of the Lord must not strive; but be gentle unto all men, apt to teach, patient; in meekness instructing those that oppose themselves; if God peradventure will give them repentance to the acknowledging of the truth."* This is a powerful statement...*in meekness instructing those that oppose themselves.* It is the meekness of Christ that can bring them to repentance through the truth. *John 16:13: "Howbeit when he, the Spirit of truth, is come, he will guide you into all truth..."*

Another point of instruction is found in Galatians 6:1: *"Brethren, if a man be overtaken in a fault, ye which are spiritual, restore such a one in the spirit of meekness; considering thyself, lest thou also be tempted."* This principle is profound. Perhaps you, like I, have seen the dreadful consequences of a situation where someone was "overtaken in a fault" and a church member's attempts to correct were not done in a spirit of meekness. Then those who were attempting to correct someone else were "overtaken in a fault."

I remember the story of someone who voted in church board meeting that some young people who had gotten into some trouble be dropped from church membership. Not long afterwards, this person's child got into the very same trouble. It is the meekness of Christ in us that can keep us from such devastating relationship situations.

Sometimes, Christians equate meekness with being a doormat to the world. This may be due to the confusion of meekness as something you do rather than something Christ is within us. Christ's meekness in us may have some manifestations that are not typically thought of as meek.

Christ was meek, yet He cleansed the temple two times. Some saw this as arrogance and blasphemy. For others, it was a relief. Christ's meekness in us may challenge us. This does not mean that we have a license to cleanse the temple. It means that as you are observed doing the Father's business, others may not perceive your actions as meek. There were probably many who did not think Peter and Paul were meek. We sometimes judge others to be less than meek when they do not do things our way, or think as we think, etc.

John 3:30: Meekness is *"He must increase; but I must decrease."* If we could but faintly understand the power of these words, we might begin to feel the power of Divinity overshadowing humanity. Like Mary, we could say, "Be it unto the handmaid of the Lord." And like Mary, that which is conceived in us and of which we give birth is of Heaven. We simply become the recipient, the vessel, for Heaven's creation process.

Talk about Divine paradoxes. Partner John the Baptist's comment: He must increase; but I must decrease with *"Blessed are the meek for they shall inherit the earth"* Matt. 5:5. And let's link Psalm 37:11 with these thoughts also: *"But the meek shall inherit the earth and shall delight themselves in the abundance of peace."* This is a great example of why we should put verse upon verse and precept upon precept. From the standpoint of our physical creation, God took some earth, shaped it, and breathed into the breath of life. Man became a living soul. This same earth that is the human part of our existence is partnered with the breath of God that is the Divine part of our experience.

Earth became the Mary, the vessel, into which Divinity breathed into existence a human being. An inheritance is something that has come down through the family. The meek receive the earth as their inheritance. They no longer live under the curse of *"from dust thou wast taken and to dust thou shalt return."* The inheritance of the earth is a reversal of the curse. The meekness of Christ helps us in every aspect of life. In the mountain top experiences, the meekness of Christ remains humble and grateful. In the pit of despair, the meekness of Christ remains submissive and responsive. His strength is made perfect in our weakness. Praise God!

Love...when I know that I am loved
and that I am a loving and lovable child of God,
then I can have *joy.*

When I have joy (in God and in myself),
I am satisfied and trust God with everyone and everything.
I have *peace.*

When my expectations are in line with reality
and I trust God with my own process and that of other people,
I have *patience.*

When Christ's peace remains in me, and patience follows peace,
then *kindness* that is real and honest can manifest.

When kindness is not outcome driven, when Christ is my heart's desire,
I will be a *faithful steward* of what is important to Him.

When I am faithfully stewarding the gifts of God
and the lessons of God,
trusting Him to be God over everything, the *meekness* of God
will manifest in me as He lives in me from the place of
"Thy will be done."

Chapter 14

THE FRUIT OF THE SPIRIT IS TEMPERANCE

I will use Webster's archaic definition of temper as a foundation for observations on temperance.

Temper: to make suitable by mingling with some other quality in proper proportions. Because temperance is often called self-control, it is easy to get too much of self into the process and the end result is less than suitable! Webster defines self-control as: control of oneself or of one's own emotions, desires, actions, etc. Webster defines temperance as: self-restraint in conduct, expression, indulgence of appetites, moderation

Let us return to 2 Peter 1:5 – 7 "*...add to your faith virtue; and to virtue knowledge; and to knowledge temperance; and to temperance patience; and to patience godliness, and to godliness brotherly kindness; and to brotherly kindness charity."*

Using Webster's archaic definition of temper (to make suitable by mingling with some other quality in proper proportions) I will suggest that temperance is a mingling of knowledge and patience. This is a spiritual alchemy directed by the Holy Spirit. Without God's word (knowledge), we have no basis for being concerned about the mastery of extremes.

Knowledge without patience leaves us with an inability to master that which we know is wrong.

Without this spiritual alchemy, we live from a man-centered works orientation. With the Spirit's blending of knowledge and patience, the resulting temperance is a heavenly gift that moves us into a God-centered, God-directed work in our lives. Looking again at the 2 Peter reference, it seems that each fruit is added to another fruit. Again, it seems to me that the order is significant suggesting a blending of fruit...almost as if to say that you cannot have just one of them, or that one is not more important than the other.

Acts 24:25 is an interesting scripture that mentions temperance. Paul is reasoning with Felix. "And as he reasoned of righteousness, temperance, and judgment to come, Felix trembled, and answered, Go thy way for this time, when I have a convenient season, I will call for thee." I believe that these words are the summation of Paul's presentation of the sanctuary service to Felix. In these words, Paul takes him from righteousness obtained by an offering in the court yard, to temperance (knowledge plus patience) learned in the holy place, to judgment in the most holy place. Paul is giving Felix the plan of salvation.

I find it very interesting that of all the gifts of the spirit that Paul could have chosen, he chose temperance. Perhaps he chose temperance because it was what Felix most needed. He was a powerful man who could do as he pleased. Felix is also hoping to be financially compensated for freeing Paul. Again, an unfulfilled appetite for money may have been one of the reasons that Paul chose temperance. It may also have been that Paul saw temperance as a part of every one of the fruit of the Spirit. Notice that the Holy Spirit's fruit is singular. Often, we speak of them as plural, but they are singular. This is significant to us.

In the Galatians 5 listing of the fruit, temperance is the last one listed. I have always felt that the order was significant, and perhaps it is in part that without temperance (knowledge plus patience) you do not have the ability to master the extremes in your life. Those extremes are the opposite of the fruit of the spirit. Temperance (knowledge plus patience) says something to us about being satisfied. When we are not satisfied, we are in want, greedy, envious, jealous, etc.

In my own journey, I have come to realize that one of the most important reasons for me to come away and be alone with God is so I can hear what my mind is thinking. I do not mean thoughts like what is for dinner. I mean thoughts about other people and situations. For instance, one morning I found myself "defending" myself in my mind. A situation had developed and I responded as I felt that I should. Now, I found myself defending that position. When I asked the Lord about my neediness or wounding that compelled me to do this, He showed me that part of my programming included the lie: if I change others will be happy. That is a huge program for many people. Seeking to please others can become a place of idolatry when it goes against your integrity and what you believe the Bible says.

The opposite of that: if they change, I will be happy, is just as harmful. What is our price? For Judas, it was thirty pieces of silver. God has called us to be His. It is as simple as that. Anything or any one asking us to be something other than what we are to be in God is wrong. During the day, if I find that I am thinking thoughts that show me I have put myself up for sale, I need to ask God "what is my neediness or wound?" It is not about that stuff out there. It is about me believing a lie. My programming needs changing.

God has entrusted us with the power of choice. We can be mastered by the things we choose, or we can, by the power of the Holy Spirit, allow the Spirit to master our power of choice, our free will. Everything depends on the right action of the will. We have always had the power of choice. It has always been ours to exercise. We make our decisions and in time our decisions make us. Making decisions inclines us to make similar decisions... this is how the heart becomes soft or hard. We are making choices and our choices are making us...making one choice eliminates many others.

Science is showing that through the neuro-pathways (plasticity principle) of the brain, our free choices are creating the person we are. Just because your past have been stolen/compromised, does not mean that you have no choices in regard to your future. Genetic inheritance plus every choice I have ever made creates ME. There is no other person like ME. Freedom of choice (willpower) exercised towards God creates a life that that becomes an act of worship.

As we recognize that our thoughts and behaviors are showing us where we need redemption's healing, we can take those thoughts and behaviors captive into Christ's obedience, and we can immediately use a prayer process and be set free. My favorite prayer process embraces the physical, emotional, and spiritual aspects of prayer. It brings healing to all parts of me. By yielding up our power of choice, we align ourselves with Heaven's power. Through constant surrender to God, we are enabled to live the new life even the life of faith. This is not a destination. It is a process.

Love...when I know that I am loved
and that I am a loving and lovable child of God,
then I can have *joy.*

When I have joy (in God and in myself),
I am satisfied and trust God with everyone and everything.
I have *peace.*

When my expectations are in line with reality
and I trust God with my own process and that of other people,
I have ***patience.***

When Christ's peace remains in me, and patience follows peace,
then ***kindness*** that is real and honest can manifest.

When kindness is not outcome driven, when Christ is my heart's desire,
I will be a ***faithful steward*** of what is important to Him.

When I am faithfully stewarding the gifts of God
and the lessons of God, trusting Him to be God over everything,
the ***meekness*** of God will manifest in me as He lives in me
from the place of "Thy will be done."

When I live from the place of "Thy will be done,"
the Holy Spirit who knows the mind and will of God
gifts me with ***temperance*** which is the mingling of knowledge
and patience to help me manage the extremes of life.

Chapter 15

ACKNOWLEDGING THAT WE NEED HELP

*A*ll healing processes require a first step: an acknowledgement that help is needed. This realization usually comes after we have crashed and burned and given up on ourselves. That we cannot do this process by ourselves has become very obvious. To this point, personal effort has not created the required changes. Freedom is needed. Part of the freedom is freedom from self.

In our personal assessments, we are not totally honest with ourselves about ourselves. We do not see ourselves as we are. Prior to the crash and burn part of our experience, we have been created in the image of man. This is done through parental modeling, the performance mode that is our learning experience, family inheritance, and through observation. Not only do we receive this environmental inheritance, we receive a physical, emotional, and spiritual inheritance. It, too, is a part of our being created in the image of man.

The wonderful opportunity in the crash and burn part of our lives is that we have an opportunity to walk away from that creation and embrace a new creation...being re-created in God's original intent for us. Behavior in the pre-crash phase of our journey has been based on lies, the unconscious beliefs that we have embraced as we have experienced the hardness of life. These are things like: I'm bad, or stupid, or ugly, or I cannot do anything right, etc.

The behavior that we manifest is probably not our core emotion...it is the symptom. This confuses us and others. Anger may be driven by grief or fear. Grief may be due to suppressed anger. Fear/anxiety may have a core of grief. There are other possible combinations, too. For too many years, the strategy has been to change the behavior...control the behavior. This truly does not address the pain. Behavior modification is a man-centered approach that does not create healing.

The emotional pain is a directional sign pointing us to the lies that we believe. Living our lives from a foundation of lies causes us to be reactive rather than proactive. These lies drive our inappropriate responses to life's situations. Most of the time we know that the way we have been living is not working. As mentioned earlier, I often hear: "Where is my victory?" We are not left without answers! "Being filled by the fruit of righteousness which are by Jesus Christ, unto the glory and praise of God" Phillipians 1:11. We can be filled BY Jesus Christ. We are to be filled BY the fruit of righteousness which are BY Jesus Christ for the glory and praise of God.

Notice the word "by." This is an interesting choice. Usually, we think of being filled *with*...not by. What does this word suggest to us? My heart always goes to the sanctuary service to help me sort out these types of questions. In the holy place is the table of shewbread holding the bread and wine, the menorah (seven-branched candlestick), and the altar of incense. The holy place work symbolizes not only the work of Christ as priest and savior, but the process of "beholding" that He invites us into. This process could also be called "abiding."

The sanctuary not only modeled the entire plan of salvation and the roles of Christ, God, and the Holy Spirit, it models the "how to" of Philippians 2:12 and 13. This shows us our part in the equation of working out your own salvation...allowing the Holy Spirit to do the sanctification process. I am so glad for verse 13 that says that it is God who worketh in you to both will and do. What we have to do is behold the Lamb. By this beholding we are changed, 2 Corinthians 3:18. How do you behold the Lamb? Basically, we have to be in the Word if we are going to behold the Lamb.

The purpose of Bible study is that we will know the truth and be able to examine ourselves accordingly. *John 8:31, 32 says, "...if ye continue in my word, then are ye my disciples indeed; and ye shall know the truth and the truth shall make you free."* Being made free doesn't necessarily mean that learning the truth will be fun or comfortable. We believe so many things that we think are true. They, however, may not be grounded in truth. We do not easily give up on what we think is true even when the facts are put in front of us. Truth encounters, like the cock crowing the third time, can be heartbreaking and they are always life changing.

> *1 Corinthians 11:28-32: "But let a man examine himself and so let him eat of that bread, and drink of that cup. For he that eateth and drinketh unworthily, eateth and drinketh damnation to himself,* ***not discerning the Lord's body.*** *For this cause many are weak and sickly among you, and many sleep (die).* ***For if we would judge ourselves, we should not be judged. But when we are judged, we are chastened of the Lord, that we should not be condemned with the world."***

Although the above is guidance given for communion service, it has wonderful application for our daily lives and our devotional processes. We behold the Lamb of God. We internalize the Bread of Life. We begin to make application of the blood and body of the Lamb. In this text, it says: not discerning the Lord's body. He wants us to understand something about the Lord's body. And because we do not, we are sick and die....physically, emotionally, and spiritually. This is very strong counsel. Sitting down with the Bible is another type of communion meal. What are our Christ lessons?

Sometimes I hold a piece of communion bread in my hand and hold it up to God. I ask: what is the lesson of the bread that you want me to know today? How may I rightly discern the Lord's body and His work for me. I do the same with a small amount of grape juice. One day I had my hands wrapped around a goblet with a small amount of grape juice in it. I asked, "Lord, what is the lesson of the blood today?" Very quickly I heard Him say, "Always keep your hands wrapped around the blood of Christ. It changes everything." Indeed, it does!

There is a difference between *accepting* the work of the cross (court-yard...Christ died once and for all), and *embracing* the work of the blood...dying daily through the power of the blood. As I see it, this is actually a filling BY Jesus. It is the oneness that He asked of the Father in John 17, *and there is a blessing pronounced over those who hunger and thirst. Matthew 5:6: "Blessed are those who hunger and thirst for righteousness, for they shall be filled."*

As we stand in the holy place, the light from the candlestick enhances our vision. By beholding, we are changed. The sanctuary was in the middle of the camp, and symbolized a God who wanted to dwell "in the midst" of His people. It is an example of Heaven's work for us so that we may be changed from our image to God's image and live in that "fullness of the Godhead" spoken of in Romans 8. My soon coming book, <u>Meeting God in His Sanctuary,</u> is a deeper presentation of the sanctuary study. The Bible is written in sanctuary language. The more you understand the sanctuary service, the more you will understand what the rest of the Bible is saying. The following scripture, for instance, becomes so powerful when recognized as a walk through the sanctuary with God for the purpose of our transformation.

> *"For this reason I bow my knees to the Father of our Lord Jesus Christ, from whom the whole family in heaven and earth is named, that He would grant you according to the riches of His glory, to be strengthened with might through His Spirit in **the inner man,** that Christ may dwell in your hearts through faith; that you, being rooted and grounded in love, may be able to comprehend with all the saints what is the width and length and depth and height—to know the love of Christ which passes knowledge; that you may be filled with all the fullness of God. Now to Him who is able to do exceedingly abundantly above all that we ask or think, according to the power that works in us, to Him be glory in the church by Christ Jesus to all generations, forever and ever. Amen" Ephesians 3:14-21.*

The power that is in the above text is astounding! The power that is available to us through the Holy Spirit is humbling. The starting place is to seek first the kingdom of God and His righteousness and the end of it all is a powerful journey of transformation that restores us to relationship living. It is a return to the garden. It is the kingdom of God within. It is a mutual indwelling. Praise God!

A primary question for each of us is the question that Job asked in Job 21:15, *"What is the Almighty, that we should serve him? And what profit should we have, if we pray unto him?"* These are good questions. They are questions that we each have probably asked ourselves. Some other good questions are what does it mean to be in the will of God, what is expected of me, and what is God looking for and how do I know where to begin? Another important consideration is learning how to make the Scriptures something that helps us get through the daily stuff of life.

Does the word of God have any application for our lives today? If so, how do we get from where we are to where we would like to be: living daily by the word of God? I am grateful that God's word has given us a starting place. "*Seek ye first the Kingdom of God and His righteousness, and all "these things" shall be added unto you*" Matt. 6:33. This scripture gives us "the end." It is the kingdom of God. What I have come to understand is that "the kingdom of God" is not just a place. It is a work. Study the kingdom parables. These are not talking about a place that is in heaven. Another definition for the kingdom of God is "a work of Divine grace upon the heart."

Now, read the above scripture this way: Seek ye first the work of Divine grace upon the heart, and all these things shall be added unto you. This offers us a totally different perspective on the text. And, for me, it makes it easier to wrap my head around the daily, practical stuff of life and how that can be a part of God's work of grace upon our hearts. The word grace (which means God's unmerited favor) can also imply the work of the Holy Spirit. So, this scripture can also be read as "the work of the Holy Spirit upon the heart."

Bible study and prayer are the elements of romance in our relationship with God. He pursues us. We pursue Him. We want to understand and know Him better...and in truth. Start with the end in mind. This principle is applicable for planning the day, a project, a goal, a relationship endeavor, our spiritual growth, our physical healing, our emotional wellness, and anything else.

God has His own plans for us. Romans 8 tells us that He plans that we be conformed into the image of the Son. He started with this end in mind.

His plans were sabotaged. He had to initiate His emergency plan that was established before the foundation of the world. These are good lessons for us. God had an ideal. God had to reach His ideal in a more difficult way after sin entered into the picture. We often have ideals, but living life in a sinful world makes things more difficult.

Sometimes we feel like we are lost and everything is hopeless. This is the best time to go back to the beginning and "Seek first the work of grace upon the heart..." No matter the job, the trial, the life lesson, the hardship, the assignment, the relationship issue, this work puts everything else into perspective. It can also help us see where we are trying to be God in our own lives. Luke 18:8 asks this question: When He (Jesus) comes, will He find faith in the land? Isn't it good news to know what Heaven considers as MOST important? Faith...what do I really believe about God?

Am I living in fear? I think that the human condition is driven by fear. "The Lord is my Shepherd I shall not want." God's word has to become flesh in our lives. When I wake up at three in the morning trying to "fix" everything, I have moved from the sheepfold. I am not trusting in the Shepherd. I do not say this to add to anyone's anxiety or guilt about being where they are right now. The beauty in God's process is that all these places are showing us our wounds. There is a way of healing and victory!

Am I living in poverty mode....greedily holding on to things and ideas as if there are no others to be had? What does this say about my belief in a God of abundance who owns the cattle on a thousand hills? Am I living as if I'm an orphan...feeling insecure, hopeless, and abandoned? What does this say about my belief in God and my understanding of what the scripture says about who I am in God? We must make the word of God "flesh" in our lives. Not only will we know the truth, but we will be empowered to walk in truth and be changed by beholding. Bible study and meditation is our first work each day.

Below is a wonderful quote from a favorite author, and it encourages me by defining meditation. In the sanctuary service we have a visual aid that models the plan of salvation, the roles of Christ, the work of Christ, and much more. One of the lessons that I have learned from the sanctuary is that the emblems representing Christ and His work can really speak to us when we ask God to give us "our daily bread" in the meaning of these things. What does He want us to know today? It is a sweet communion.

One thing this whole process has taught me is that a devotional time, or a Bible study time can be a part of this communion, but it does not take the place of it. I want to have God speak to me about the things of life. This is how the entire process finds application and meaning for this present life.

"Meditation is the activity of calling to mind, and thinking over, and dwelling on, and applying to oneself, the various things that one knows about the works and ways and purposes and promises of God. It is an activity of holy thought, consciously performed in the presence of God, under the eye of God, by the help of God, as a means of communion with God.

Its purpose is to clear one's mental and spiritual vision of God, and to let His truth make its full and proper impact on one's mind and heart. It is a matter of talking to oneself about God and oneself; it is, indeed, often a matter of arguing with oneself, reasoning oneself out of moods of doubt and unbelief into a clear apprehension of God's power and grace.

Its effect is ever to humble us, as we contemplate God's greatness and glory and our own littleness and sinfulness, and to encourage and

reassure us—comfort us, in the old, strong, Bible sense of the word—
as we contemplate the unsearchable riches of divine mercy displayed
in the Lord Jesus Christ." Knowing God, J. I. Packer, page 23

Praise God for this counsel. Meditation and contemplation are not emptying the mind. They are a filling up of the mind with the mind of God which He shares with us in His word and by inspiration of the Holy Spirit impressing upon us great truths. In all of this, we begin renewing the mind and this beholding changes everything.

Chapter 16

IT IS JUST THE BEGINNING...

cannot bring myself to entitle this page "conclusion." It seems just too final for me. For one thing, I do not think that you ever get to the end of God and His word. For another thing, I have observed in the several years of writing this document, that my points-of-view change. Is that not great?! I am glad that I can change my perception of things. I have read and studied the Bible all my life, and it keeps opening up. I find this exciting. It is a living Word. I encourage you to keep at your study, prayer, meditation.

One thing that helps me to go deeper in my Bible study is that I study the stories from several dimensions. I share this with you in the hopes that you, too, will find this approach to be an extra tool that you put in your Bible study tool kit.

- This is a real story about real people. What life lessons are available in this story?
- This story is like a parable...what does it say symbolically?
- This story is a snapshot of the entire great controversy...what part of the picture is portrayed in this story? What life lessons are here? What do I learn about this cosmic struggle?

- This story is about relationship issues...relationship with God, self, and others. What can be learned in this context?
- In Bible history portrayed as you read individual chapters, how are they building upon each other? How do the sins of the fathers play out? How is our time much like theirs?

There is much we could share with each other, and my hope is that this book will inspire you in your worship, study, love and praise of God. I think there could be no greater thing said of any book!

Blessings,
Linda

PS: On our website (www.leasnhs.com) you will find a collection of additional writing in the section called "A Cup of Tea." This may also be a blessing to you. You can also contact us through that website if we can be of assistance to you on your journey. Let us know if you would like to be on our mailing list so you can know of upcoming classes or seminars.

The Fruit of the Spirit
The Kingdom of God Within

Love...when I know that I am loved
and that I am a loving and lovable child of God,
then I can have *joy.*

When I have joy (in God and in myself),
I am satisfied and trust God with everyone and everything.
I have *peace.*

When my expectations are in line with reality
and I trust God with my own process and that of other people,
I have *patience.*

When Christ's peace remains in me, and patience follows peace,
then *kindness* that is real and honest can manifest.

When kindness is not outcome driven, when Christ is my heart's desire,
I will be a *faithful steward* of what is important to Him.

When I am faithfully stewarding the gifts of God and the lessons of
God, trusting Him to be God over everything, the *meekness* of God will
manifest in me as He lives in me from the place of "Thy will be done."

When I live from the place of "Thy will be done,"
the Holy Spirit who knows the mind and will of God gifts me
with *temperance* which is the mingling of knowledge and
patience to help me manage the extremes of life and
discern between good and evil.

But now being made free from sin,
and become servants to God,
ye have your fruit unto holiness,
and the end everlasting life.
Romans 6:22

GOALS FOR A CUP OF TEA STUDIES:

- Transforming: My assignment in life is to share information. We must consider the information that we receive and decide if we are interested in allowing that information to have a transforming power in our lives. My prayer is that in this study we will each be transformed.

- Modeling: There is a golden thread of love and beauty and power that runs through all of Scripture. These thoughts marry Old Testament with New Testament, and uses God's symbolism in the Old Testament sanctuary service as a model for understanding the entire process of sanctification...being filled with the fruit of the Holy Spirit...being changed from our image to God's image.

- Restoring: These studies put the Spirit's filling us with God's fruit, into the context of Eden lost to Eden restored; Eden being symbolic of our relationship with God.

- Applying: We must learn how to reprogram our minds with God's words and God's processes. The battle is for the mind. This is a matter of life and death.

- Understanding: How we can weave Bible study and prayer into our daily lives so that we learn to use God's precious promises for our overcoming?

How do we see God? How do we see ourselves as children of God? Our answers can help us daily, as each day holds the potential for experiences that include Gethsemane, Calvary, the Tomb, and resurrection. Some days, it may feel like we have been given a crash course...like the Job experience.

CPSIA information can be obtained at www.ICGtesting.com
Printed in the USA
LVOW12s0758150514

385625LV00004B/5/P

9 781629 525600